THE WISDOM OF
MAIMONIDES

Other Books by Edward Hoffman

Despite All Odds: The Story of Lubavitch

*The Heavenly Ladder: Kabbalistic Techniques
of Inner Growth*

The Hebrew Alphabet: A Mystical Journey

Jewish Holiday and Sabbath Journal

Jewish Wisdom: A Journal

*My Bar/Bat Mitzvah: A Memory
and Keepsake Journal*

*Opening the Inner Gates: New Paths
in Kabbalah and Psychology*

Sparks of Light: Counseling in the Hasidic Tradition
(coauthored with Zalman M. Schachter-Shalomi)

*The Way of Splendor: Jewish Mysticism
and Modern Psychology*

THE WISDOM OF
MAIMONIDES

The Life and Writings
of the Jewish Sage

EDITED BY

Edward Hoffman, PhD

TRUMPETER

BOSTON & LONDON · 2008

Trumpeter Books
An imprint of Shambhala Publications, Inc.
Horticultural Hall
300 Massachusetts Avenue
Boston, Massachusetts 02115
www.shambhala.com

9 8 7 6 5 4 3 2 1

First Edition
Printed in the United States of America

☻ This edition is printed on acid-free paper that meets the
American National Standards Institute z39.48 Standard.
Distributed in the United States by Random House, Inc.,
and in Canada by Random House of Canada Ltd
DESIGNED BY DEDE CUMMINGS DESIGNS

Library of Congress Cataloging-in-Publication Data

Maimonides, Moses, 1135–1204
[Selections. English. 2008]
The wisdom of Maimonides: the life and writings of the
Jewish sage / edited by Edward Hoffman.—1st ed.
p.   cm.
Includes bibliographical references.
ISBN 978-1-59030-517-1 (pbk.: alk. paper)
1. Judaism—Works to 1900. 2. Maimonides, Moses,
1135–1204—Anecdotes. I. Hoffman, Edward II. Title.
BM545.A2513 2008
296.1'81—dc22
2007041843

For my children,
Jeremy, Aaron, and Daniel

CONTENTS

PART THREE

Visionary Tales

125

PREFACE

I FIRST LEARNED of Maimonides when I was five years old. It was the school year's opening day at the New York City yeshiva where I was starting first grade uneasily, for my parents were not observant. My maternal grandfather was the famous cantor Louis Lipitz, raised in Kiev—and descended from generations of prominent cantors and Jewish educators. He had insisted that I receive full-time religious instruction, and Zichron Moshe was only a twenty-minute walk away in our crowded city neighborhood. Until that day, I had never attended school but had already learned to read from my parents, both dedicated public school teachers.

Soon after our class was seated that September morning, the rabbi distributed to each of us a Hebrew primer, a prayer book, a *Fun with Dick and Jane* reader, and a thin notebook. Its blue cover portrayed a slender, thoughtful bearded man of indeterminate age who wore a turban—Maimonides. The picture was intriguing. His identity as an enduring leader of Judaism was explained to us later that week, as was the purpose of the notebook that bore his visage: to master the sacred Hebrew alphabet.

Though I was a quick learner in virtually all subjects, Hebrew calligraphy was my nemesis. Initially I nearly failed it, despite my most valiant efforts. Repeatedly try as I would, I simply could not consistently draw those twenty-two ancient letters legibly. Every morning for years as I took out that blue notebook for in-class Hebrew writing exercises—and every evening as I practiced again in graded homework— Maimonides seemed to gaze at me with silent reproach. In his eyes, I felt inadequate, and I didn't like the feeling.

Later, while majoring in psychology at Cornell University, I eagerly continued my Jewish education. In studying Maimonides' momentous *Guide for the Perplexed* for a Western philosophy course, I learned that he ranked among history's greatest thinkers, whose influence since his death in 1204 remained truly ecumenical and global—transcending its origins in medieval Jewish rationalism. He remained a compelling pedant for the ages.

Indeed, I found Maimonides' ideas on emotional self-mastery to be quite relevant for my courses on personality and social psychology. For example, his emphasis on the role of habit in shaping human conduct seemed remarkably contemporary, as did his view on the negative effects of chronic anger, worry, and sadness on individual health. In some respects, his provocative ideas—such as nurturing states of higher consciousness—even seemed ahead of the mainstream psychology I was absorbing from my professors.

Immersing myself in Maimonides' biography, I was fascinated by his upbringing in Spain's Golden Age with its vibrant Christian, Jewish, and Muslim interplay. I found myself dreaming of castles in Spain and Moorish parapets overlooking verdant lands. To my surprise, I also discovered that the iconic portrait engraved in my childhood mind was only a mid-eighteenth-century imagining of Maimonides' appearance— not at all a true picture. This made immediate sense, for I knew that as a rabbinic teacher, he certainly would have endorsed the age-old Jewish prohibition against human image making, including his own. Nobody really knew what Maimonides had looked like. This knowledge was both satisfying and liberating. In a mysterious way, I now felt empowered to use my own imagination about this creative giant—who wrote so intriguingly about self-development, ethical behavior, and prophecy. The impassive, unsmiling figure associated with my Hebrew notebook struggles was not the real Jewish sage honored by our tradition for more than eight hundred years. Somehow, this awareness allowed me to see Maimonides in a new, encouraging light—one that has continued to illumine my own work to the present day.

In producing this anthology, my purpose has been to acquaint readers with Maimonides' colorful life and especially to highlight some of his wide-ranging teachings from my vantage point as a psychologist interested in the spiritual aspects of our existence. For not only as a brilliant rabbinic scholar but also as a busy practicing physician to Egypt's royal court, Maimonides was keenly interested in how mind, body, and spirit are closely interwoven for all. Through his diverse Judaic and medical treatises, he offered practical advice that powerfully resonates with today's interest in wellness and longevity.

I hasten to add that this book is in no way intended to be all-inclusive. For example, in selecting among Maimonides' extensive Judaic precepts, I have tried to highlight those which he regarded as paramount—and also those which are more obscure yet fascinating precisely for their premodern sensibility. Nor is this anthology designed to minimize the considerable body of scholarly achievement devoted to Maimonides' wide-ranging work. Certainly each year sees the publication of new volumes around the world that explore his memorable life and achievements. Undoubtedly the tremendous growth in scholarly attention to Islam has spurred interest in his unique challenges and accomplishments in living as a devout Jew in the Muslim world.

Rather, *The Wisdom of Maimonides* today is meant as a bridge to the complex landscape—both intellectual and cultural—that has always surrounded his vast legacy. If this book accomplishes that goal, it will have fulfilled its purpose.

EDITOR'S NOTE

I N PRESENTING Maimonides' writings in English translation—all composed originally in either Judeo-Arabic
or Hebrew more than eight hundred years ago—I have
relied mainly on existing translations and then rendered
their English into a more contemporary style for improved
readability. These have primarily included Yale University's
multi-decade translation of the *Mishneh Torah;* Friedlander's
translation of *The Guide for the Perplexed;* Gordon's translation
of *The Preservation of Youth;* Twersky's anthology, *A Maimonides
Reader;* Stiskin's *Letters of Maimonides;* Weiss' and Buttersworth's
Ethical Writings of Maimonides; and Alexander's and Romano's
Once Upon a Time . . . Maimonides. I have also used this method
in presenting the tales about his momentous life. As we know
from a famous letter to his own translator, Maimonides advised
that translations always be guided by the principle of clarity
rather than strict literalness. My intent has been to follow
Maimonides' guidance.

The issue of translating gender terms is more challenging,
in that the Jewish law of Maimonides' era clearly differentiated

between men and women. To a large extent, Orthodox Judaism in most variants today maintains these distinctions—indeed based partly on Maimonides' own codifications. Therefore, when presenting his views specifically on Jewish practice, I have kept his gender construction. In all other instances—such as when Maimonides wrote about ethics, prophecy, self-improvement, or mind-body health—I have sought to use gender-neutral phrasing while remaining faithful to his conciseness.

ACKNOWLEDGMENTS

THIS BOOK would not have been possible without the valuable help of others. Editor Jennie Cohen of the *National Jewish Post & Opinion* provided the initial impetus for this project by publishing my article on Maimonides and mind-body medicine. From the outset, my editor, Beth Frankl, at Shambhala Publications has been a constant source of encouragement and guidance. My oldest son, Jeremy, has been a font of both enthusiasm and advice while pursuing rabbinic training in Israel. Conversing with my teenage son Aaron about Jewish history and philosophy has been gratifying.

I have enjoyed stimulating conversations with Rabbi Niles Goldstein, Rabbi Neal Kaunfer, Aaron Hostyk, Paul Palnik, Rabbi Zalman M. Schachter-Shalomi, and Howard Schwartz relating to topics in this book.

Above all, I would like to thank my wife, Elaine, for her patience and unflagging support throughout this project.

PART ONE

MAIMONIDES

A Concise Biography

The Jewish World in 1200

Area of Jewish settlement
◉ Major place of Jewish settlement
• Other place of Jewish settlement
–·–·– Limit of Islamic rule
–··–··– Limit of Christian rule

0   1,000
km

KINGDOM OF ENGLAND · Dublin · London
KINGDOM OF FRANCE · Rouen · Paris · Troyes · Lyons · Marseilles
GERMAN EMPIRE · Cologne · Mainz · Worms · Speyer · Nuremburg
KINGDOM OF POLAND · Breslau
RUSSIAN PRINCIPALITIES · Kiev
KINGDOM OF HUNGARY
BULGARIAN EMPIRE · Constantinople · Salonica · Thebes
KINGDOM OF SICILY · Rome · Naples · Salerno · Melfi · Otranto · Palermo · Sicily · Sardinia · Malta
Barcelona · Toledo
ALMOHAD EMPIRE · Fez · Tripoli · Barka
Crete · Cyprus
SELJUK SULTANATE OF ICONIUM
GEORGIA · Derbent · Tabriz · **AZERBAIJAN** · **ARMENIA** · Amadia
Aleppo · Damascus · Hamadan · Okbara · Isfahan · Shiraz
SHAHDOM OF KHWARIZM · Ghazni
Samarkand · Khotan
ABBASID CALIPHATE · Baghdad · Pumbeditha · Hillah · Basra · Mosul
AYYUBID SULTANATE · Alexandria · Cairo · **HEJAZ** · **ARABIA**
YEMEN · Aden
ABYSSINIA
River Nile
River Indus · River Ganges
SULTANATE OF DELHI
INDIA · Malabar Coast · Ceylon
Bay of Bengal
Arabian Sea
Indian Ocean
Mediterranean Sea

Muslim Spain

Mediterranean Sea

Balearic Islands

Atlantic Ocean

NAVARRE

Besalú

CATALONIA

Barcelona
Balaguer
Lérida
Tarragona
Tortosa
Barbastro
Monzón
Jaca
Ruesta
Huesca
ARAGON
Saragossa
Tarazona
Alagón
Daroca
Catalayud
Tudela
Vitoria
Estella
Miranda
de Ebro
Belorado
Logroño
Nájera
Ágreda
Soria
Sigüenza

VALENCIA

Valencia
Denia

Castrojeriz
Burgos
Castrillo
San Cristóbal
de Entreviñas
Sahagún
León

CASTILE

Guadalajara
Alcalá de Henares
Madrid
Escalona
Toledo
Uclés
Talvera
de la
Reina

ANDALUSIA

Cordoba
Jaén
Cabra
Lucena
Carmona
Seville
Niebla
Málaga
Ronda
Algeciras

GRANADA

Baza
Guadix
Granada
Pechina
Almería

PORTUGAL

Coimbra
Santarém
Lisbon
Évora
Beja
Badajoz
Mérida

0   100
km

THE LIFE OF MOSES MAIMONIDES

U NDOUBTEDLY, the most influential and celebrated of all Jewish philosophers is Maimonides (Moses ben Maimon).* Over the course of his colorful lifetime, Maimonides (1138–1204) became renowned throughout the world as a scholar, rabbinic thinker, and communal leader. At the same time, he achieved international acclaim as a physician to the royal family in Cairo and as the author of key medical texts. Though legends have surrounded Maimonides' inspiring life for more than eight hundred years, its main aspects are sufficiently clear for understanding his powerful legacy.

---

* In Judaism, he is traditionally revered as the Rambam, an abbreviation of the words "Rabbi Moses ben Maimon."

EARLY LIFE AND WANDERINGS

Moses ben Maimon was born in Córdoba, the capital of Andalusia (Muslim Spain). Ruled for a century by the relatively tolerant Almoravid dynasty, it was Europe's largest and most affluent city. As both a cultural and a political center, Córdoba boasted a multitude of libraries and observatories, mosques, madrasas (colleges), and hospitals—enticing scholars throughout the eastern Islamic world. Home to diverse ethnic groups and cultures, it also provided an exciting cosmopolitan ambience. Later known historically as Spain's Golden Age, this was an era in which Jews enjoyed safety and freedom to a degree unprecedented in their existence outside the Holy Land. They also contributed actively to Andalusian politics, culture, science, medicine, and commerce.

Within Córdoba, most Jews, including Moses and his family, resided in the Jewish Quarter, a comfortable locale. Wealthier homes usually encompassed several levels, a private courtyard with fountain and pools, a well-tended garden, a library, and a servant area. Moses's father, Rabbi Maimon ben Joseph, was a renowned communal leader and physician who traced his lineage back through many distinguished generations. It's therefore likely that his family lived in relative luxury.

Because legal documents and family letters in that epoch rarely mentioned women even by name, almost nothing is known historically about Moses's mother. By most accounts, she died in childbirth, and Rabbi Maimon later remarried. His second wife, also historically nameless, gave birth to a son, David, who grew up emotionally close with Moses, and apparently three daughters; only one of their names, Miriam, is known.

In accordance with custom, Rabbi Maimon educated both his sons at home. This we know directly from Maimonides, who later reminisced, "First reading I learned from my father and teacher—may his memory be blessed—who learned it from his own rabbi." Reflecting his father's erudition, Moses studied a curriculum whose girth would amaze modern educators. Its Jewish component included the Hebrew Bible, Mishnah, Talmud, and related codes and commentaries, and its secular subjects incorporated astronomy, logic, mathematics, optics, law, and rhetoric.

Young Maimonides, whose education was supplemented by rabbinic tutors, also precociously sought out Rabbi Maimon's medical texts detailing herbs, poisons, and surgical methods. The only subject he seemed to have disliked was poetry—both Hebraic and Arabic. Indeed, throughout Maimonides' prolific writing, he preferred to express himself in terse prose rather than utilize flowery imagery. Aside from book learning, it's likely that Moses as oldest son also gained knowledge by observing his father's Judeo-judicial, literary, medical, and communal activities.

All this came to an abrupt end when Moses was nine years old. During the previous quarter century, a Berber confederation had arisen in Morocco's Atlas Mountains. It was led by a charismatic religious zealot, Abdallah ibn Tumart, who in 1121 proclaimed himself the Madhi—"the divinely inspired one." Preaching a purified, ascetic form of Islam that many Berbers found appealing, he proclaimed a jihad against the more tolerant Almoravid Muslim dynasty. When Ibn Tumart died in 1130, the movement's leadership passed to his chief aide, Abd al-Mumin. Swelled by increasing adherents, his forces in 1147 conquered the Moroccan capital of Marrakech and then immediately launched an invasion of Andalusia. Their rallying cries were "No church and no synagogue!" and "Death to the infidels!" The following year, they seized control of Córdoba.

For the Almohads (whose name derives from the Arabic phrase "those who affirm the Oneness of God"), Christianity and Judaism were diabolical. Synagogues were therefore destroyed and Jewish schools shut down. An Almohad commentator of the time expressed outrage that in places like Córdoba, Jews actually "had become so bold as to wear Muslim clothing and mingle with Muslims in external affairs." That affront was soon remedied, for Jews were forced to wear distinctive garb, and both Christians and Jews were severely pressured to convert.

Faced with the choice of apostasy or death, the Maimon family—like many others—was forced into a weary exile. Seeking Jewish refuge in one devastated city after another, they wandered across southern Spain for nearly twelve years. Aside from a sojourn in the southeastern port city of Almería, until it too fell to the Almohads in 1151, Rabbi Maimon's family left few clues about its precise whereabouts or activities for future historians to uncover. Legend has it that during this period, young Maimonides encountered the renowned Arabic philosopher-physician Averroës (1126–1198), who had similarly fled Córdoba to escape Almohad persecution. Although these two great medieval thinkers shared many viewpoints about medicine, science, and faith, they almost certainly never actually met.

Though Maimonides' youth was outwardly unstable, he succeeded in advancing both his education and his scholarly pursuits. By his early twenties, he had already written two books, which together revealed his immense talent for methodical thinking. The first, known in Hebrew as *Ma'amar ha-Ibbur,* provided a practical guide to the complexities of the Hebrew calendar, which is lunar based. The second, *Treatise on the Art of Logic,* was addressed to a Muslim—either real or fictional—and presented a concise overview of logical terminology. Containing no references to Judaism, the treatise relied heavily on the work of Alfarabi (ca. 870–950), an influential Arabic philosopher steeped in Aristotle.

MOROCCAN SOJOURN

In 1159 Rabbi Maimon immigrated with his family to Fez. Why he chose to settle in this foreboding, inland Moroccan walled city—then suffering under its fourteenth year of oppressive Almohad rule—is unclear. However, Fez had many respected libraries and academies, and ties between Fez and Córdoba Jewry had been strong for centuries. It's probable that Rabbi Maimon had personal connections with leaders of Fez's beleaguered Jewish community and therefore hoped to secure a permanent home for his family at last.

Deciding against both exile and martyrdom, the majority of Fez Jews had outwardly converted to Islam, but they often continued to practice their ancestral religion secretly at home. It was a dangerous strategy, for those who were caught faced the certain penalty of death. However desperate, this seemed the best way for Judaism to survive—and surely one day safely reemerge into open observance.

Such was the view expressed by Maimonides in his famous *Letter of Consolation,* composed around 1160. It was initiated as a rebuttal to a prominent Moroccan rabbi's call for Jewish martyrdom over pseudoconversion to Islam. Maimonides insisted that Judaism valued preserving life above all other choices—and consequently, "Even if one worships idols under duress, his soul will not be cut off." Significantly, he urged struggling Jews everywhere to undertake exile rather than choose pseudoconversion or martyrdom: "What I should like to suggest to all of my friends and everyone who consults me is to leave these places and go to where you can practice your religion and fulfill the Torah's precepts without compulsion or fear. . . . We are guided by the admonition of the sages not to dwell in a city in which there are fewer than ten righteous residents. . . . You will surely find peace, [as] the world is sufficiently large and extensive."

This epistle, boldly lambasting a much older, well-placed rabbi, was a remarkable act of leadership from a still-unknown scholar in his midtwenties, and it effectively saved Morocco's Jewry from utter disintegration. This successful initiative also foreshadowed Maimonides' ascension seven years later to appointed leadership of Egypt's Jewish community, and eventually he became unofficial head of his era's entire Jewish world.

Scholars today vigorously debate whether the Maimon family itself publicly converted to Islam in Fez to avoid the threat of execution. If so, the act would not have been unusual at all—and would certainly have been consistent with Maimonides' acceptance of pseudoconversion to Islam as Jewishly legitimate, as his *Letter of Consolation* had contended. The evidence is definitely suggestive but still inconclusive.

During Maimonides' five years in Fez, he expanded his rabbinic learning and also received formal medical training from Jewish and Arab physicians. In this regard, he was closely following his father's own career path. Maimonides also continued writing his *Commentary on the Mishnah*. A monumental task, it involved reproducing this entire sacred text of ethics and law and appending his interpretation. Consuming ten years of scholarship, it would help establish its author as a preeminent Jewish thinker.

Most likely the Maimon family would have maintained its fragile existence in Fez if not for calamitous political change in 1163. The Almohads' longtime caliph, Abd al-Mumin, suddenly died, and his successor, Abu Yakub Yusuf, accelerated persecution of Jews throughout his dominion. With escalating violence, religious authorities under Yakub Yusuf's command routed out pseudoconverts to Islam for mandated punishment.

Perhaps the most prominent among these was Rabbi Judah ibn Shoshan, beloved friend of the Maimon family and Maimonides' personal tutor. Convicted of relapsing to Judaism, he was tortured to death in 1165. Maimonides was arrested and charged with the same crime. If not for the intervention of his scholarly Muslim friend Abul Arab ibn Moisha, the punishment would have been identical. Maimonides was temporarily released from jail, but rearrest and conviction seemed only a matter of time. And so the Maimon family decided to flee Morocco and find refuge in the Holy Land.

After escaping from Fez at night, Maimonides and his brethren hid themselves during daylight hours and then traveled after dark for several days. They safely reached the outskirts of Ceuta, a bustling coastal town in northern Morocco. There, at night, the Maimon family found an inn in which to hide once more before they could book ship's passage. Stealthily boarding on a dark Saturday night in April 1165, the Maimon family expected to reach the Holy Land's port of Acre in about a month's time.

During the first two weeks the voyage was pleasant enough, and Maimonides worked diligently on his *Commentary on the Mishnah*. Suddenly, a severe storm struck and all aboard faced imminent drowning as their ship tossed wildly. Panicked by the raging sea, the crew jettisoned the cargo overboard—a common practice in that time. As Maimonides reminisced in a letter years later, he calmed his fear, prayed for deliverance, and vowed that should they survive, he would institute—in commemoration of God's compassion—two annual fast days "for my family and all my household, and to order my descendants to keep these fasts also in future generations and give charity in accordance with their means. I further vowed to observe a day in seclusion and devote it to prayer and study. For on that day, God alone was with me on the sea. So, upon the yearly return of that day, I do not wish to be in human society—unless I am compelled."

FROM ACRE TO ALEXANDRIA

It may seem surprising that the Maimon family sojourned only a year in the Holy Land after their desperate escape, but Jewish communal life there proved disappointing and dismal. Indeed, it had been that way—poor and disorganized—ever since the Romans had annihilated the Jewish national state almost precisely a millennium earlier. Only a few thousand dispirited Jews lived in the entire land, under hostile Christian rule since the First Crusade culminated triumphantly in 1099. For sixty-five years, Jerusalem had been ruled by a succession of Frankish kings, the latest being Almaric 1.

Comprising scarcely two hundred families, Acre's Jewish community was nevertheless Judaism's bastion in the Holy Land. Acre's well-known rabbinic leader, Jaffet ben Eliyahu, was warm and welcoming to the Maimon family and even accompanied them on their pilgrimage to Jewish holy sites. But he had little tangible to offer them concerning either livelihood or financial stability.

To be sure, Maimonides spent several days exploring Jerusalem, praying at the Second Temple's Western Wall and visiting other holy sites, including the Cave of the Patriarchs in Hebron. He was fascinated by the Judean landscape and the architecture of ancient buildings. Yet he understood that adequate sources of income for Jews in the Holy Land were virtually nonexistent and acquiesced in his father's unwavering decision to relocate once more, this time in Egypt.

And so, in mid-1166, Maimonides and his family arrived in Alexandria—an international, cosmopolitan city of that era. As a hub of Mediterranean commerce as well as culture, it offered more than twenty centers of higher learning—the most famous of which was the Academy of Aristotle, built just outside the city.

In Alexandria prospects quickly seemed to brighten for the

Maimon family. David married soon after their arrival. Establishing himself as a traveling jewel merchant, he went into business with his older brother—who apparently served as a supportive "silent partner" while continuing his scholarly activities on a full-time basis. Why Maimonides at nearly thirty was still unmarried has long puzzled historians; it was certainly atypical for educated Jewish contemporaries. There seems no supportive evidence to back the claim that he actually married as a young man but became a childless widower—and then remarried in midlife.

When Rabbi Maimon died of illness not long after relocating the family to Alexandria, both his sons grieved tremendously. They received numerous letters of condolence from all over the Jewish world recalling his erudition and kindness. Had the last eighteen years of Rabbi Maimon's life not been spent in hapless wandering with his family around the Mediterranean region, he might well have achieved historical influence closer to that of his famous son.

MOURNING AND SUCCESS IN EGYPT

Mainly for economic reasons, David and Moses decided to move once more—this time to Fustat (Fostat). It was a pleasant, residential city about two miles from Cairo, which housed the seat of Egypt's administration, including the caliph's court, troops, harem and entourage, and the many menials who served them. With access to both the Mediterranean Sea and the Indian Ocean, Fustat was favorably situated for international commerce. Its geographic position was especially advantageous for the India trade in which many Jewish merchants, including David and Moses Maimonides, were involved.

For more than two centuries, Egypt had been ruled by the relatively liberal Fatimid dynasty, and Cairo was a bustling city of religious and secular study. The Fatimid caliphs encouraged

literary activity, composed poetry, and promoted the decora-
tive arts. The famous al-Azhar Mosque—a longstanding religious institution—offered free public education and even
classes for women. Together with Baghdad in the East and
Córdoba in the West, Cairo ranked among the Islamic world's
greatest cultural centers.

Offering several synagogues, Maimonides' neighborhood
comprised mostly Jews living among Christians and a smaller
Muslim population. He and David's family shared a comfortable house; they dressed and ate well. The synagogue to which
they belonged was a short walk from home. Whether Rabbi
Maimon's daughters were still present, or had married and
moved elsewhere, is unknown.

In this peaceful milieu, Maimonides' life seemed to sta-
bilize at last. He received remuneration for lecturing on secular subjects, including mathematics, logic, and astronomy, and
continued to work on his *Commentary on the Mishnah*. Contrary to many Jewish contemporaries, he firmly opposed receiving payment for any Torah-guided activity, whether
teaching, writing, or communal work. It's therefore likely that
he assisted David in business affairs to bolster the family
income.

If Maimonides as an ardent scholar had indeed involved
himself in commerce during his early Fustat years, it would
hardly have seemed unusual. Several decades earlier, the renowned Spanish poet-physician Judah Halevi had maintained
close ties with merchants and even engaged in trade. Indeed,
many Jewish traders were admired scholars, and the merchant-
scholar was becoming an ideal for this era.

However, Maimonides' major focus was undoubtedly
Judaic writing, and in 1168 he finally completed *Commentary
on the Mishnah*. It had been an immense, decade-long project.
In the introduction, Maimonides highlighted the importance
of the Oral Law (derived from the Mishnah and later the Tal-

mud) as it pertained to Judaism's prophetic and legalistic traditions. He deemed this topic vital to undermining the Karaite sect's theology.

For, arising some three centuries earlier, the Karaites considered themselves "true Jews" who accepted only the Bible's legitimacy for guiding daily life. Much to rabbinic consternation, they completely rejected the Mishnah and Talmud, the foundation for Judaism's millennia-old Oral Law. Though the Karaite sect never came close to supplanting rabbinic Judaism, thinkers like Maimonides worried about its impact in undermining Jewish unity and communal cohesiveness.

The *Commentary on the Mishnah* included two supplementary sections, both of which became conceptual bulwarks of Judaism for centuries through to the present day. The first was his introduction to Perek Herek, the last chapter of the Babylonian Talmud's tractate *Sanhedrin*. It contains the cryptic statement, "All Jews have a share in the World to Come." Maimonides not only intriguingly presented his view of the afterlife as a wholly transcendental realm but also specified Judaism's bedrock principles—what have become known ever since as the Thirteen Articles of Faith—including monotheism, prophecy, revelation, the authority of the Torah, divine reward and punishment, and the messianic era.

The second supplementary section was his introduction to *Pirkey Avot* (Ethics of the Fathers), the ancient foundation text of Jewish ethics. In a tract that later came to be known simply as *The Eight Chapters,* Maimonides drew upon Aristotelian teachings as well as Judaic insights in essentially producing a manual on how to become a sage. Much of the work stressed the importance of daily habit and self-analysis—especially relating to emotions—as the keys to inner development. Encouraging and optimistic, Maimonides contended that virtually all persons can enhance their character and well-being by following specific guidelines.

Oddly enough, *Commentary on the Mishnah* initially attracted little attention. Perhaps the subject matter was insufficiently captivating or controversial to spark wide interest. To be sure, the erudite work increased Maimonides' stature in intellectual circles and the local Egyptian Jewish community—but it did not make him famous. Explorer-writer Rabbi Benjamin of Tudela, who visited Fustat about the time of the *Commentary*'s publication, always made sure to chronicle Jewish celebrities wherever he roamed. He said nothing about Maimonides at all.

However, during the next several years, Maimonides' reputation for integrity coupled with scholastic brilliance climbed steadily. In 1171 he was appointed *nagid* (grand rabbi) of Egypt's entire Jewish community, an influential position for which he refused salary and which he subsequently held at various times throughout later life. As *nagid,* Maimonides served as Jewish judicial leader, issuing binding legal opinions on cases involving marriage, divorce, inheritance, synagogue activity, and related matters. He also appointed rabbinic judges for localities and supervised Jewish communal officials throughout the region.

Most scholars today believe that Maimonides—only thirty-three years old and still single when he became *nagid*—gained this prestigious post partly because of political connections: specifically with al-Kadi Fadil ("The Excellent Judge al-Fadil"), Saladin's chief administrator. For, almost simultaneous with Maimonides' sudden elevation in 1171 to Jewish communal leadership, Saladin—the ambitious nephew of Syria's potentate Nureddin—became sultan over all Egypt. Raised in a prominent Kurdish family, Saladin was virtually the same age as Maimonides and shared his admiration for intellectual-religious achievement. Though it's unknown precisely when they first met, legends have circulated for centuries about their enduring friendship.

With his love for Jewish scholarship, it's not surprising that Maimonides would soon embark on a new, strikingly more ambitious project: a codification of all major Jewish law into a single readable work. At the time, many centuries of Jewish legal opinion lay scattered haphazardly among thousands of pages of Talmudic text and related commentaries.

Initially, it seems, Maimonides intended only to produce a personal study guide to Talmudic rulings, but as the project steadily took shape and grew, his goal similarly expanded. Known as the *Mishneh Torah* (literally, Second Torah, or Repetition of the Torah), it would similarly consume a decade of scholarly labor. But unlike his *Commentary on the Mishnah,* it would generate both intense acclaim and heated controversy.

As Maimonides' rabbinic reputation expanded beyond Egypt's borders, Jews from far-flung communities all over the globe sought him out in person or wrote him letters for advice on religious, social, and political matters. He busily composed responsa and gave counsel when asked.

Among his most famous epistles, written in 1172, was one to Yemenite Jewry. Suffering the anguish of forced conversion to Islam with no reprieve in sight, the demoralized community was on the verge of collapsing. Jacob Alfayumi, its rabbinic leader, desperately sought Maimonides' guidance. Responding empathically but calmly, Maimonides placed Jewish Yemenite persecution within a wider historical context and then invoked the prophets' assurance of future redemption: steadfast faith would always triumph over adversity and eventually lead to the Messianic Age.

"May God, who created the world with the attribute of mercy, grant us to behold the ingathering of the exiles to the portion of His inheritance, contemplate His graciousness, and to visit early in His Temple," Maimonides urged at the end of his epistle. "Peace, peace, as the light shines—and much peace until the moon be no more."

Maimonides' heartfelt support proved effective in rallying Yemenite Jewry, but his own stamina would be sorely tested when tragedy struck in 1174. His beloved brother, David, was drowned in the Indian Ocean while voyaging on business—and with him was lost the entire family fortune in the form of jewels he had been carrying for trade. A successful merchant, David had gladly supported Moses as well as his own family; the two men had always been extremely close.

A grief-stricken Maimonides fell into near collapse both physically and mentally. He may have suffered a mild heart attack, and for nearly a year he spent much of his time lying weakly in bed and accomplishing little. In a letter later written to Rabbi Jaffet ben Eliyahu of Acre, Maimonides recalled:

> The greatest misfortune to befall me in all my life was the death of my righteous brother. He went down in the Indian Sea, and with him was lost our own property and that of others as well. His little daughter and his widow remained in my care. When the bad news arrived, I became ill and depressed for a whole year; I thought I was lost. Eight years have passed; I am still in mourning and cannot find consolation. I brought him up: he was my brother and my student. He conducted business and earned our livelihood. He was versed in the Talmud, the Bible, and the field of grammar. I had no greater joy than seeing him. Whenever I behold his handwriting or one of his books, my sorrow renews itself. If not the study of Torah, which is my delight, if not the study of the sciences, which helps me overcome my grief, I would be lost.

After his brother's death, Maimonides was obliged to shoulder monetary responsibilities for the first time in his life. His scholastic and communal activities would have to make room for financial considerations. With meager savings left, he had few options. Almost certainly the prospect of taking over David's jewelry trade held minimal appeal. Maimonides had never been interested in becoming a full-time merchant. He had always abhorred the extensive travel that it necessitated, and after his brother's tragic death, such activity was unthinkable.

And so Maimonides chose a new career entirely: that of practicing physician. True to his character, he applied to this seemingly secular discipline his same qualities of uncompromising integrity, meticulous scholarship, and spiritual sensitivity.

It cannot be determined precisely how Maimonides acquired his medical knowledge. Almost certainly its origins lay in his early broad education, encompassing astronomy, logic, mathematics, philosophy, botany, and medicine—all of which derived from classic Greek thought. Of course, Rabbi Maimon was himself a practicing physician who may have encouraged young Moses's intellectual interest in the discipline. It's likely, therefore, that his study of Galen and Hippocrates began in youth and continued through his Mediterranean wanderings.

Some medical historians suggest that Maimonides first conducted "hands-on" treatment when living in Fez during the mid-1160s. However, it seems equally plausible that he never had clinical instruction until opening his own practice in Fustat. Indeed, many Muslim physicians at the time considered the study of classic medical texts to be wholly adequate preparation for direct patient care.

Over the next few years, Maimonides' reputation as a healer blossomed. Marriage at age thirty-seven, in 1175, and subsequent fatherhood must have bolstered his emotional security. As is true for Maimonides' mother, the names of his wife and daughter (who died in infancy) are historically unknown; his other child, Abraham, grew up to become a renowned rabbi-physician in his own right.

Maimonides' father-in-law was Mishael Halevi of Fustat, an advisor in Saladin's royal court—and the father of five sons and probably several daughters as well. A leading figure in Fustat's Jewish upper class, Mishael Halevi came from a distinguished family of scholars and international merchants. He was also undoubtedly well positioned to promote his new son-in-law's fledgling medical practice.

This was a profession that Maimonides viewed as a sacred duty—one that required complete devotion. Rabbi Maimon had undoubtedly served as a key role model in this regard, for Maimonides later declared that "the study of medicine has a very great influence upon the acquisition of the moral virtues and of the knowledge of God, as well as upon the attainment of true spiritual happiness. Therefore, its study and acquisition are preeminently important religious activities."

As a physician, Maimonides zealously kept abreast of all the latest medical discoveries and critically examined the great medical texts of the past. Rejecting popular belief in astrology, amulets, and magical potions as cure-alls, he insisted that treatment of illness demands a comprehensive knowledge of the human mind and body. In direct contrast to many of his medical colleagues, he downplayed the importance of drugs and surgery and instead argued that diet, exercise, and mental outlook are the key determinants of day-to-day health. He also related various physical ailments—including asthma and digestive disorders—to specific emotional imbalances such as chronic worry, sadness, and anger.

Not surprisingly, Maimonides' bold and creative approach to healing eventually attracted the notice of the royal family in nearby Cairo. In 1187, about a dozen years after opening his practice, he became court physician to Saladin's vizier and confidant al-Kadi al-Fadil, the most influential person in Egypt. Well read and extraordinarily energetic, al-Fadil had effectively advised several Fatimid rulers before serving Sultan Saladin. Maimonides soon became celebrated in this official and salaried post, gaining many prominent Muslim families as patients. When King Richard the Lionheart of England visited the region, he asked Maimonides to become his personal physician. Preferring, like his father, to live under Islamic rather than Christian domination, he declined the offer. It's fascinating to speculate how subsequent Jewish history—especially in Europe—might have altered had he agreed to relocate with his family to England.

While dedicating himself to a burgeoning medical practice, Maimonides nevertheless continued his philosophical and religious involvements. In 1180 he finally completed his *Mishneh Torah*—having worked on it intermittently for ten years, though not in sequence, completing its different sections at different times. Unquestionably recognizing its colossal scope, Maimonides confidently asserted in his introduction:

> Ours is a time of great disasters. Everyone feels the stress of the present hour. The wisdom of our wise is lost, and the counsel of our scholars is hidden. . . . Therefore, the commentaries, codes, and decisions of the sages, which they thought to be generally intelligible, are not understood in our days—only a few are able to comprehend these perfectly. . . . Therefore, I, Moses ben Maimon from Spain, trusting in God . . . decided to compile the conclusions to be deduced from all the compilations and commentaries pertaining to all the laws of the Torah. This presentation is put forward in simple style and a concise manner, so that the Oral Law may become familiar to all.

Composed in an elegant Hebrew, the *Mishneh Torah* sum-
marized all of existing Jewish law—not only for the Diaspora
but also for an independent State of Israel. This dual format
reflected Maimonides' belief that the Messianic Age would
begin in 1216—within the lifetime of many contemporaries,
and that its reborn Jewish state would need a lucid constitution for effective governance.

In Hebrew, the alternative title for the *Mishneh Torah* is *Yad
ha-Hazakah* (The Mighty Hand)—based on the last words of
the Pentateuch: "and in that mighty hand, and in all the great
terror that Moses showed in the sight of all Israel." Because the
numerical value of the Hebrew word *yad* is fourteen, Maimonides divided his magnum opus into fourteen sections of
differing length.

Presented as a complete legal code, it basically set forth the
final decision of all major Jewish laws—in Hebrew language
that was precise, vigorous, and easily understandable. Whether
motivated by the desire for literary clarity and brevity or—as
his critics fiercely contended—shameless self-promotion, Maimonides credited no sources in compiling his *Mishneh Torah*.
He did not even note diverging rabbinic opinions and debate
on key questions of Jewish law. In a religious tradition that
honored differing viewpoints and citing one's teachers, Maimonides had therefore produced something that, for some, was
arrogantly worthless.

Overwhelmingly, though, Maimonides gained tremendous
praise for accomplishing the *Mishneh Torah*. It was extolled
throughout the Jewish world as an astounding landmark
achievement—far more consistent with the attainment of a
team of notable rabbinic scholars laboring for generations than
the production of one individual working on many other
tasks at the same time. It also transformed the entire landscape
of subsequent rabbinic literature. Not for another four hundred years—until the 1565 publication of Rabbi Joseph Caro's

Shulkhan Arukh (The Prepared Table)—would an effective replacement come into widely accepted usage. Even then, and continuing through the present day, the *Mishneh Torah* would rank among the most important Jewish texts ever written—alongside the sacred Mishnah and Talmud.

INTERNATIONAL JEWISH LEADER

Maimonides was soon catapulted to Jewish leadership far beyond Egypt's borders and venerated as the foremost rabbinic authority of his time. More than ever before, diverse queries for his legal opinion came to Fustat from throughout the Jewish world. Letters arrived from rabbis, scholars, judges, teachers, heads of academies—and even from private citizens who requested an official responsum. Wanting to preserve religious accessibility to those lacking wealth or prominence, Maimonides personally replied to every letter; he deliberately refused to hire an aide for this purpose. Not everyone was answered with equal promptness or detail, but all were greeted politely and empathically.

Perhaps inspired at age forty-eight by the birth of his son, Abraham, the previous year, Maimonides began writing the third of his most important works—*Guide for the Perplexed*. It was dedicated to Joseph ibn Aknin, who had studied philosophy previously with a Muslim teacher. Joseph had survived as a forced convert to Islam during the Almohad persecutions until seizing an opportunity to escape successfully to Alexandria. From there he had sent letters and poetic compositions to an impressed Maimonides, who in 1185 invited Joseph to study with him in Fustat. The young scholar did so for two years in close association. Then, at age twenty-five, he relocated to Allepo, Syria, where he would become a prominent rabbi-physician. Maimonides continued to teach by correspondence and then began sending chapters of the *Guide* in the form of an extended epistle—addressed to Joseph and those like him.

What was its purpose? Certainly Maimonides was eager to mentor those sincerely seeking his ethical and religious guidance. Strongly rejecting the rampant superstitions of his day, he sought to educate a new generation—and those to follow—motivated by intellectual curiosity, devotion to truth, and spiritual awareness. As Maimonides later explained in the introduction to the *Guide,* his aim was explicit: "And when these gates [of my book] are opened and these places are entered into, souls will find rest therein; their eyes will be delighted, and their bodies will be eased of their toil and labor."

Though viewed as a rationalist by his contemporaries for rejecting divination and astrology as nonsense, Maimonides believed strongly in the reality of realms beyond our mundane perceptions. He felt that most people make use of only a small fraction of their higher potential for transcendent experience, and therefore prescribed specific steps by which any individual could attain divine communication: in a real sense, become a prophet.

For example, Maimonides declared, "If a person, perfect in his intellectual and moral faculties, and also perfect—as far as possible—in his imaginative faculty, prepares himself [properly] . . . he must become a prophet, for prophecy is a natural state of humanity."

During the same momentous year of 1187, Maimonides suddenly found himself close to death by Muslim decree. He was charged with relapsing to Judaism, and it ironically sprang from his old friend and former savior, Abul Arab ibn Moisha. Traveling from Fez on business, he was astounded to discover that Maimonides had not only abandoned Islamic practice but had come to occupy the Jewish community's highest position.

Ibn Moisha was angry enough to report Maimonides to the authorities and demand a tribunal. If convicted, Maimonides would certainly be executed. Fortunately, Maimonides' chief judge was his royal friend and patient al-Fadil. Unable to alter Muslim law regarding apostasy, the vizier cleverly ruled that Maimonides had never actually converted to Islam in his youth but had merely worn extravagant garb—hence, the accusation of his relapsing to Judaism was false and invalid. There the matter ended.

Maimonides steadily composed the *Guide* in Judeo-Arabic, unlike his two earlier major works, both written in Hebrew. Immediately after appearing in 1190, it sparked huge interest, and became his best-known and most influential work. In attempting to synthesize the best of Greek philosophy with Jewish theology in the search for ultimate truth, the work had few literary rivals. Especially after its translation into Latin and then contemporary European languages, it inspired people of diverse faiths with its optimism and lucidity.

Among educated Jews everywhere, the *Guide* enhanced Maimonides' already formidable reputation. In far-off southern France, sages in Lunel requested a copy in Hebrew, since they could not read Arabic. Maimonides replied that he hadn't time to undertake a translation, and so the task fell to young Samuel ibn Tibbon—himself a scholar and the son of another well-known scholar. He wrote to Maimonides for permission to begin work, and the two corresponded frequently about the project.

When Ibn Tibbon asked if he might visit Maimonides in Fustat to collaborate more effectively, he received a vivid reply in 1195. As Maimonides' most famous personal letter, it appears in countless literary anthologies. "All you will gain by your visit will be to take a glimpse at me. You should not expect to discuss with me even one scholarly topic or to spend with me one hour during the day or the night," Maimonides cautioned his younger colleague. "Let me give you an account of my daily routine:

I live in Fustat, the Sultan lives in Cairo, and between
the two places are two Sabbath zones. The tasks I have
to perform at the court of the Sultan are rather onerous.
I must visit him every morning under any circumstances. When he does not feel well, or when one of his
children or wives is ill, I cannot leave Cairo but must stay
in the palace for the greater part of the day. It also frequently happens that one or two officials are ill, and I
must attend them. In short, early every morning I leave
for Cairo and, if nothing extraordinary happens, I return
to Fustat in the afternoon—never earlier.

Hungry I arrive and find all the rooms crowded with
people: Jews and non-Jews, distinguished persons and
plain folk, judges, officials, friends and foes alike, who
await the time of my return. I dismount, wash my hands,
and beseech them kindly to wait while I have something
to eat, my only meal of the day. Then I treat them and
dispense prescriptions for their cure.

The coming and going of patients lasts until the
evening. I assure you, sometimes it is eight o'clock and
later before I am through speaking to them all and giving them their orders. Because of extreme fatigue I must
lie down on my back, and when night falls, I cannot
speak for exhaustion. . . . Such is my daily routine.

Owing mainly to Maimonides' declining health, the *Guide*
was his last major opus. He continued, however, to produce
many smaller works on Jewish philosophy or law. Among the
most famous was his *Letter on Resurrection,* composed in 1191.
It served as a rebuttal to Rabbi Samuel ben Eli, head of Baghdad's renowned Torah academy, who accused Maimonides of
rejecting traditional Jewish faith in resurrection.

Ben Eli seems to have personally disliked Maimonides and
feared his mounting influence throughout the Jewish world.

As a result, he may have concocted this charge as a way to safe-guard his own status as rabbinic authority and eliminate a possible rival. The allegation had serious implications not only for Jewish theology but also for Maimonides, as it could have entangled him with Muslim political and religious authorities. During the same year, the renowned Islamic philosopher Shihab ad-Din as-Suhrawardi had been executed for heresy, including denial of resurrection.

Thus, in a letter to his protégé Joseph ibn Aknin—addressee of the recently completed *Guide*—Maimonides publicly affirmed his belief in a literal resurrection and noted its listing among his Thirteen Articles of Faith, penned nearly a quarter century earlier. As its author had hoped, this letter effectively squelched Ben Eli's attempt to disgrace and possibly destroy his esteemed rabbinic opponent.

When Saladin died in 1193, his empire fell into contention among feuding family members. Al-Afdal, Saladin's eldest son, became ruler of Syria, and, enjoying friendship since youth with Maimonides, eventually sought practical advice for health improvement. In a remarkable 1198 treatise known today as *The Preservation of Youth* (or, *Regimen of Health*) Maimonides provided guidance on how al-Afdal might enhance his physical, emotional, and spiritual well-being for maximum vigor and longevity. The overall perspective predated by many centuries seemingly innovative concepts today involving mind-body medicine, such as the link between mood and physical illness.

By then Maimonides was close to sixty years of age and already experiencing a noticeable decline in his own vitality. Nevertheless, he still managed to compose several more medical treatises and supervise translations of his diverse writings into Hebrew. After the year 1200, Maimonides produced no more books but continued to write responsa and maintain an active correspondence. Until his death in December 1204, mentoring and tutoring his teenage son, Abraham, an enthusiastic learner, provided a special source of parental joy.

Maimonides' insights on ethics and law have exerted a profound influence upon Judaism for centuries. His books on health, medicine, and philosophy became classics for people of all religious paths and backgrounds. As the popular rabbinic saying has long declared, "From the time of Moses to the time of Moses Maimonides, there has arisen none like this Moses."

PART TWO

SELECTED

WRITINGS

I

UNDERSTANDING
HUMAN PERSONALITY

To be sure, Maimonides lived in a distant era when the advent of scientific psychology lay nearly seven hundred years in the future. To all available knowledge, neither he nor any other medievalist—whether Christian, Jewish, or Muslim—conducted any empirical study of emotions and behavior. Yet, based mainly on Hebraic and ancient Greek sources, Rabbi Moses ben Maimon had much to say about human personality. From our perspective, he would certainly have regarded himself as a psychological thinker—one especially concerned with why people act as they do.

Though conceding the role of heredity, Maimonides far more decisively emphasized the role of environment in shaping our adult personality. In this regard, he accentuated Judaism's longstanding view—clearly articulated in *Pirkey Avot*

(Ethics of the Fathers)—that we are all extremely susceptible to social influences. Throughout his extensive writings, he stressed the importance of associating with sages and the wise—and, if necessary, paying for their presence in one's everyday affairs.

Conversely, Rabbi Moses ben Maimon warned repeatedly against mingling with unethical and mean-spirited people and advised voluntary exile if their presence could not be effectively avoided. Having been forced to lead a troubled, nomadic life owing to religious persecution, he undoubtedly spoke from heartfelt conviction when he vividly and almost poignantly declared, "If one is unable to go to a city with good customs, he shall dwell alone in solitude . . . ; [if necessary], he shall go off to the caves, the briers, or the desert, and not accustom himself to the [wrong] way."

Maimonides often commented, too, on the tremendous effects of habit on our personality formation. Centuries before William James, as the founder of American psychology, made his famous pronouncement in 1890 on habit as "the fly-wheel of society," Maimonides saw this force as inestimable in its importance for our own proper development. He also elaborated on how we can make specific use of habit to fortify our character. His ideas strikingly parallel the insights of modern behavioral psychology, for he recommended repetition as a key device.

As a physician, Maimonides viewed mind and body as significantly connected. He saw human emotion as a powerful force that, if unbridled, could wreak havoc upon an individual's overall health. For this reason he regarded emotional self-control as an ideal and prescribed ways for strengthening it. Again, habituation was the key for creating a healthy personality: it's not good intentions but, rather, countless tiny and seemingly insignificant actions that really count in everyday life.

TEACHINGS

Ordinary Human Consciousness

Know that just as the blind person cannot imagine color, as the deaf person cannot experience sounds, and as the eunuch cannot feel sexual desire, so bodies cannot attain spiritual delights. Like fish, who do not know what is the element of fire, because they live in its opposite, the element of water— so are the delights of the spiritual world unknown in this material world.

We enjoy only bodily pleasures, which come to us through our physical senses, such as those of eating, drinking, and sexual activity. Other levels of delight are not present to our experience. We neither recognize nor grasp them at first thought. They come to us only after great searching. It could hardly be otherwise, since we live in a material world. (Introduction to Perek Herek, *Sanhedrin*)

The Nature of Pleasure Seeking

If you contemplate these two forms of pleasure—physical and nonphysical—you will appreciate the baseness of the one and the supremacy of the other, even in this material world. This is obvious from the fact that most people—and perhaps even all—will expend prodigious psychological and physical effort in order to attain position and honor in the eyes of others. This pleasure is not physical pleasure, such as eating and drinking.

Similarly, many people choose to seek revenge on their enemies rather than indulge themselves in physical pleasure. And we find that many people avoid the greatest of physical pleasures out of fear that this will bring them shame and embarrassment in the eyes of people, or because they desire to enhance their reputation.

If this is our situation in the material world, surely this applies in the spiritual world—the World to Come—where our souls will be able to experience the Creator. This pleasure cannot be parceled out or described, nor can an analogy be given to define it. . . .

This is the ultimate good to which no good can be compared, nor can any pleasure be likened to it. For how can there be any comparison between that which is eternal and endless, and any temporal matter? (Introduction to Perek Herek, *Sanhedrin*)

Limits of the Human Mind

There is considerable difference between one person and another as regards [mental] faculties, as is well known to philosophers. While one person can discover a certain thing by himself, another is never able to understand it, even if taught by means of all possible expressions and metaphors and over a long period. His mind can in no way grasp it, his capacity insufficient for it. [But] this distinction is not unlimited. A boundary is undoubtedly set to the human mind that it cannot pass. (*The Guide for the Perplexed*, book 1, chapter 31)

Quests of the Mind

There are things . . . that are acknowledged to be inaccessible to human understanding, and humanity does not show any desire to comprehend them—being aware that such knowledge is impossible. For example, we do not know the number of stars in heaven, whether the number is even or odd. We do not know the number of animals, minerals, or plants and the like. There are other things, however, that humanity very much desires to know, and strenuous efforts to examine and to investigate them have been made by thinkers of all types and at all times. (*The Guide for the Perplexed,* book 1, chapter 31)

Social Influence on Traits

Undesirable traits are acquired through association with the wicked. (Commentary on *Pirkey Avot,* chapter 1)

Low Self-Worth

When a person considers himself to be wicked, he will not hesitate to transgress. There will be no sin that he will consider too severe to transgress. (Commentary on *Pirkey Avot,* chapter 2)

The Role of Habit

When the regular exercise of refined qualities precedes wisdom and a firm habit is established, the wisdom that one learns later will encourage him to maintain those positive qualities. This, in turn, will motivate him to intensify his connection with wisdom, inspiring him with a love and enthusiasm for it, for this encourages an ingrained habit.

When, by contrast, bad tendencies are ingrained before one learns wisdom, the wisdom that one learns [creates a conflict, for it] prevents a person from [indulging] the desires to which he is accustomed. This will cause him [to see wisdom] as a burden and to abandon it. (Commentary on *Pirkey Avot,* chapter 3)

Pleasure Seeking in Life

Spiritual pleasures, by contrast, are constant, never to be interrupted. There is no form of comparison between these [spiritual forms of pleasure] and [physical] pleasure. . . . Similar concepts apply when a person has refined himself and reaches such a rung [in the spiritual worlds] after his death. One will not comprehend physical pleasure and will have no desire for it. [To do so could be compared to] a powerful king leaving his kingship and going back to playing ball in the streets of the city. Although surely there was a time when he preferred to play ball rather than deal with the affairs of the kingdom, this was when he was immature and had not learned to distinguish between the nature of the two matters. In the same way, we glorify and give greater regard to the pleasures of the body than to the pleasures of the soul. (Introduction to Perek Herek, *Sanhedrin*)

The Need for Wisdom

All the great evils that people cause to each other because of certain intentions, opinions, or religious principles are due to nonexistence—because they originate in ignorance, which is the absence of wisdom. For example, a person who is blind, who has no guide, stumbles constantly because he cannot see and causes injury and harm to himself and others.

In the same manner, various classes of people—each in proportion to their ignorance—bring great evils upon themselves and other individual members of our species. This state of society is promised to us by the prophets in such words as "And the wolf shall lie down with the lamb" and "The cow and the bear shall feed together" and "The sucking child shall play on the hole of the asp" (Isaiah 11:6–8). The prophet also points out what will be the cause of this change, for he says that hatred, quarrel, and fighting will come to an end because humanity at that time will have a true knowledge of God: "They shall not hurt or destroy in all my holy mountain, for the earth shall be

full of the knowledge of the Lord as the waters cover the seas"
(Isaiah 11:9). (*The Guide for the Perplexed,* book 3, chapter 11)

———

If people possessed wisdom—which stands in the same relation to human form as sight to the eye—they would not cause
any injury to themselves or others, for the knowledge of truth
removes hatred and quarrels and also prevents natural injuries.
(*The Guide for the Perplexed,* book 3, chapter 11)

Temperament and Human Individuality

It has already been established that humans are naturally social
beings, that by virtue of their nature they seek to form communities. Humans are therefore different from other living
beings that are not compelled to combine into communities.
They are, as you know, the most complex form in creation and
therefore include the largest number of constituent elements.
This is the reason the human race contains such a huge variety of individuals that we cannot discover any two persons
exactly alike in any moral quality or in external appearance.

The basis for this reality lies in the variety of human temperament. . . . Such a variety among the individuals of our
species does not exist in any other classification of living beings, for the variety of individuality in every other species is
limited.

Only the human species forms such exceptions, as two
people may be so different from each other in every respect
that they seem to belong to two different [biological] classifi-
cations. While one person is so cruel that he kills his youngest
child in anger, another is too delicate and fainthearted to kill
even a fly or a worm. (*The Guide for the Perplexed,* book 2,
chapter 40)

Variations in Temperament

If people were exactly the same in physical constitution and temperament, they would act alike in the same set of circumstances. But dispositions vary widely, and consequently there is variety in conduct.

Human individuals are possessed of varying temperaments, differing widely one from the other to an extreme degree. Some are inflamed and in a constant state of irritation. Others are emotionally composed and hardly ever irritated, and should they be annoyed, it will be very slightly and take a long time. Some are of an extremely proud nature. Others are very humble. Some are addicted to sensuality, and their erotic appetites are never sated. And others are of a pure heart and do not long even for the few things that the body requires.

Again, there are persons so avaricious that they would not be satisfied with all the wealth in the world, but others curtail their desires and are content even with such a little that it does not suffice for their needs and do not strive to obtain all they require. Some there are who would rather afflict themselves with hunger to hoard wealth and do not spend the smallest coin on themselves without considerable pain, whereas others deliberately squander all of their possessions.

It is the same with all other dispositions—the jovial and the morose, miserly and generous, cruel and kind, fainthearted and brave. (*Mishneh Torah,* book 1, treatise 2, chapter 1:1)

We Are All Molded by Habit

We naturally like what we have been accustomed to and are attracted to it. This may be observed among villagers. Though they rarely enjoy the benefit of a douche or bath and have few enjoyments—and pass a life of privation—they dislike town life and do not desire its pleasures, preferring the humbler things to which they are accustomed to the more lavish concerning which they are strangers. It would give them no satisfaction to live in palaces, to be clothed in silk, and to indulge in baths, ointments, and perfumes.

The same is the case with those opinions to which a person has been accustomed from youth; he likes them, defends them, and shuns the opposite views. This is likewise one of the causes that prevents people from discovering truth and make them cling to their habitual patterns. (*The Guide for the Perplexed,* book 1, chapter 31)

Understanding Character

A person's virtues do not accrue in accordance with the qualitative magnitude of a single action but in accordance with the numerical magnitude of his actions. This is to say, the virtues really accrue by reason of the frequent repetition of good deeds, and thereby one attains a strong position—but not through the performance of merely one great act of goodness does one attain a strong position.

This may be illustrated by the case of an individual who gives a deserving person on a single occasion a thousand gold pieces, but to another he gives nothing. By this one great act, he does not acquire the quality of generosity as does one who donates a thousand gold pieces over a thousand occasions, giving each single piece through a generous feeling. The latter has repeated his generous act a thousand times and attained a strong position. As for the other, on only a single occasion was his heart deeply moved to perform a kind action, and after that it ceased.

Similarly, in the Torah the reward for one who redeemed a captive for a hundred dinars, or performed charity to a poor person to the extent of a hundred *dinars* (medieval coins) sufficient for his needs, is not as great as the reward for one who redeemed ten captives or supplied the needs of ten poor people, each at a cost of ten dinars. (Commentary on *Pirkey Avot,* chapter 3)

The Need for Fresh Experience

When we continually see something, however sublime, it may be that our regard for it will be lessened, and the impression we have received of it will be weakened. . . .

The sight of that to which a person has been accustomed for a long time does not produce such an ardent desire for its enjoyment as is produced by objects new in form and character. (*The Guide for the Perplexed,* book 3, chapters 47, 49)

Be Careful about the Company You Keep

The human individual is created in such a way that one's character and actions are influenced by neighbors and friends, and one follows the customs of the people in his country. Therefore, one must associate with the just and the wise continually, in order to learn from their actions, and keep away from the wicked, who walk in darkness, to avoid learning from their actions. That is what Solomon said: "He who walks with wise men will become wise, but he who associates with fools will become evil" (Proverbs 13:20). And it says, "Blessed is the person who does not walk in the counsel of the wicked" (Psalms 1:1). (*Mishneh Torah,* book 1, treatise 2, chapter 6:1)

Parents and Children

You asked a question concerning parents and children: Why do we state that the good fortune of children depends upon the meritorious acts of their parents? Furthermore, what benefit can accrue to the parents by virtue of their children's good deeds—considering that during the parents' lifetime their attachment to their children was only of a physical nature? To be sure, this relationship constitutes an unfathomable mystery. For in some fashion, the seeds will always retain some imprint of their forebears. (*Letter to Hasdai Ha-Levi*)

2

ON BECOMING A SAGE

THROUGHOUT Maimonides' influential life, he taught that becoming a wise and righteous person is essentially a matter of training. Though readily acknowledging the role of heredity in shaping our core personality —what today psychologists call temperament—he nevertheless believed that achieving wisdom and ethical perfection invariably resulted from following certain specific guidelines.

The more closely one observed these principles, Maimonides emphasized, the greater the likelihood of attaining beneficial results. Conversely, the less an individual heeded these admonitions concerning right conduct, the probability increased for developing a harmful lifestyle. Luck was irrelevant and certainly could not be manipulated by human acts—such as involving magic and divination. Rather, these principles, which he derived from both Judaism and Greek philosophy— especially from Aristotle—applied to everyone as he or she faced life's challenges and joys.

In this regard, Maimonides was a true antielitist who saw all human beings as coexisting on a level playing field. That is, in his cogent view, family wealth and status never guarantee a person's inner achievement. Instead, what ultimately makes the difference for each of us is our determination to follow the right path. Forced at the age of ten into hapless exile with his family, he certainly never romanticized adversity and material hardship. Yet, as a practicing physician to the Egyptian royal court, he saw enough to know that exalted social position often fails to bring either happiness or wisdom.

Specifically, Maimonides recommended that we always seek the "middle way" with respect to emotional traits: that we avoid extremes and embrace neither too great nor too meager an expression of particular feelings. "The right way is the mean in every single one of an individual's character traits," he observed. "Therefore, the wise persons of old commanded that one continuously appraise his character traits and direct them in the middle way to attain perfection."

Maimonides viewed ordinary existence as presenting us with almost endless opportunities for personal growth and wholeness. As a busy, sought-after healer, he was undoubtedly a realist who saw up close both outer and inner flaws. Yet he remained a lifelong optimist who emphasized that "one can change his character. Everything depends on free will and choice."

TEACHINGS

The Importance of Self-Motivation

There are no external motivators for divine service. Rather, it is the person himself who must turn himself to either side, as he desires. (*Eight Chapters,* chapter 8)

Maintain a Balanced Character

The right way is the mean in every single one of a man's character traits. Therefore, the wise men of old commanded that a man continuously appraise his character traits and direct them in the middle way so that he becomes perfect. (*Mishneh Torah,* book 1, treatise 2, chapter 1:4)

Personal Change Is Possible

A man can change his character. Everything depends on his free will and choice. (*Eight Chapters,* chapter 8)

Work with Dedication

Just as the employer is warned against robbing the wage of the poor workman and against delaying it, so is the poor workman warned against robbing the employer by idling away his time on the job—a little here and a little there—and wasting the entire day deceitfully. He must be scrupulous throughout the time of work. Also, he is required to work to the best of his ability—as the upright Jacob said to Rachel and Leah: "I have served your father [Laban] with all my strength" (Genesis 31:6).

For this reason, Jacob was rewarded even in this world, as it is written: "The man became exceedingly rich" (Genesis 30:43). (*Mishneh Torah,* book 13, treatise 1, chapter 13:7)

Rules for Character Development

It is in your hands to choose life and the good, for freedom of choice has been given to you. Habituate yourself to righteous conduct, for human nature depends on habit formations that are structured into the very fabric of being. (Letter on Ethics to Son, Abraham)

———

Love truth and justice and cleave unto them, for in them lies your success. You will then be like one who builds on a strong rock. Despise falsehood and injustice, and do not covet their savory delicacies, for you will be like one who is building on sand or plastering a wall with saliva. (Letter on Ethics to Son, Abraham)

———

Pursue a simple, innocent, and pure existence. (Letter on Ethics to Son, Abraham)

———

There is no greater nobility than ethical idealism and no more glorious inheritance than trustworthiness. (Letter on Ethics to Son, Abraham)

Avoid Idleness

Despise idleness and a life of ease, for they are the cause of the body's dissolution—and of impoverishment, boredom, idle talk, stubbornness, and slander. They provide a ladder, as it were, to Satan and his cohorts. (Letter on Ethics to Son, Abraham)

What Your Home Should Be

You should structure your home so that it will be a place where sages frequently gather. The distinction of one's home for this purpose should be so powerful that when one sage says to another, "Where will we meet?" the other will say, "At so-and-so's house." (Commentary on *Pirkey Avot,* chapter 1)

Avoid Arrogance

Whenever a person is haughty, the Divine Presence wails over him. (Commentary on *Pirkey Avot,* chapter 4)

———

Wisdom will not be found among the proud and the haughty. (Commentary on *Pirkey Avot,* chapter 2)

Strive for Brevity

A person should always endeavor to speak few words with much content, and not the converse. (Commentary on *Pirkey Avot,* chapter 2)

Your Actions Have Consequences

In all times and places, whoever performs a wicked act and brings about dishonesty and flaws will ultimately suffer harm from those wicked activities that he himself has spread. For he promotes the activities that will bring harm to himself and others.

Conversely, a person who promotes virtuous qualities and who brings about good deeds will ultimately derive benefit from this activity, for he has promoted doing things that will benefit himself and others. This was wisely stated in the verse "A person's labors will be his recompense" (Job 34:11). (Commentary on *Pirkey Avot,* chapter 2)

Strive for a Mentor

If you meet a highly developed person, you should make yourself flexible—serving him as he desires and devoting yourself to his service. However, if you meet a younger person, you should not do this. You should be earnest with him and need not be as flexible or as unpretentious.

Nevertheless, do not think that this warning against being unpretentious with a younger person requires you to receive him with animosity or anger. This is not so. Instead, you should receive every human being—regardless of age or station in life—with happiness and joy. This is a more [demanding charge] than Shammai's instruction, "Receive every person with a cheerful countenance." (Commentary on *Pirkey Avot*, chapter 3)

Vows Help Self-Restraint

Taking and maintaining vows to abstain from certain elements ingrains in a person the tendency to bridle the [desires] he seeks to curb. This tendency will continue, and it will be easy to acquire the quality of restraint, that is, the tendency to protect oneself from impurity. (Commentary on *Pirkey Avot*, chapter 3)

Cultivate Simplicity

All the difficulties and troubles we meet [in daily life] are due to the desire for superfluous things. When we seek unnecessary things, we have difficulty even in finding that which is essential. For the more we desire to have the superfluous, the more we meet with difficulties. Our strength and possessions are spent in unnecessary things, and we are wanting when required for that which is necessary.

Observe how Nature proves the correctness of this assertion. The more necessary a thing is for living beings, the more easily it is found and the cheaper it is. The less necessary it is, the rarer and more costly. For example, air, water, and food are indispensable for everyone. Air is most necessary, for if a person is without air for a short time, he dies, while it is possible to be without water for a day or two. Air is also undoubtedly found more easily and cheaply than water.

Water is more necessary than food, for some people can endure four or five days without food provided they have water. Water also exists in every country in larger quantities than food and is also cheaper.

The same proportion can be noticed in the different kinds of food: that which is more necessary in a certain place exists there in larger quantities and is cheaper than that which is less necessary.

No intelligent person, I think, considers musk, amber, rubies, and emeralds as very necessary for people, except as medicines, and they, as well as other like substances, can be replaced for this purpose by herbs and minerals. This shows God's kindness to His creatures, even to us weak beings. (*The Guide for the Perplexed,* book 3, chapter 12)

The Need for Mindfulness

If we pray with the motion of our lips and our face toward the wall but simultaneously think of our business;

If we read the Torah with our tongue while our heart is occupied with the building of our house, and we do not think of what we are reading;

If we perform the commandments only with our limbs;

We are like those who are engaged in digging the ground, or hewing wood in the forest, without reflecting on the nature of those acts or by whom they are commanded or what is their purpose. We must not imagine that [in this way] we attain the highest perfection. On the contrary, we are like those in reference to whom Scripture says, "You are near in their mouth, and far from their heart" (Jeremiah: 12:2). (*The Guide for the Perplexed,* book 3, chapter 51)

How to Develop Mindfulness

I will now commence to show you the way to educate and train yourselves to attain great perfection.

The first thing you must do is this: Turn your thoughts away from everything while you say the Shema or other daily prayers. Do not content yourself with being devout when you read [merely] the first verse of Shema or the first paragraph of the prayers. When you have successfully practiced this for many years, try when reading or listening to the Torah to have all of your heart and all of your thoughts occupied with understanding what you read or hear.

After some time, when you have mastered this, accustom yourself to having your mind free from all other thoughts when you read any portion of the other books of the prophets, or when you say any blessing, and to have your attention directed exclusively to the perception and understanding of what you utter.

When you have succeeded in properly performing these acts of divine service and your thoughts during their performance are entirely abstracted from worldly affairs, then take care that your thoughts be not disturbed by thinking of your wants or of unnecessary things. . . . Have your mind exclusively directed to what you are doing. (*The Guide for the Perplexed,* book 3, chapter 51)

Avoiding Anger

Anger is a most evil quality. One should keep aloof from it to the opposite extreme and train oneself not to be vexed even by a thing over which it would be legitimate to be irritated. (*Mishneh Torah,* book 2, treatise 1, chapter 2:3)

———

The life of an angry person is not truly life. The sages have therefore advised that one keep far from anger until being accustomed not to take notice even of things that provoke irritation. This is a good way. (*Mishneh Torah,* book 2, treatise 1, chapter 2:3)

The True Heroes

Those engaged in study and in absorbing philosophical habits and the moral teachings of the Torah acquire strength for their souls. They are the true heroes, as their souls are not subject to change and get very little agitated. (*The Preservation of Youth,* chapter 3)

Cultivate Self-Discipline

The more a person is disciplined, the less one is affected by both extremes—good times and bad—so that when favored by a great, worldly fortune, called by the philosophers "imaginary goodness," one does not get excited nor appear particularly great and good in one's own eyes. (*The Preservation of Youth,* chapter 3)

True Wisdom: Getting to the Essence

When a person contemplates the true essence of things and the knowledge of reality, he attains a wisdom whereby he understands that the greatest good in this world does not stay with us all of our days, because it is inferior in value—being perishable and destructible. (*The Preservation of Youth,* chapter 3)

Your Thought Has Power

For whatever one thinks that hurts him while thinking it and that brings him sadness, sighing, and mourning can be of only two kinds: either regretting what has been, as when recalling money once had and lost, or regretting the death of a person his heart grieves for, or worrying about what may happen in the future, such as that he may suffer a loss. . . .

Yet, just as it is possible that something painful, worrisome, or fearful may happen, it is also possible that because of your reliance on God, the reverse of what you feared may happen. Both what you fear and its reverse are possible. (*The Preservation of Youth,* chapter 3)

Be Willing to Relocate

If one is in a country with evil customs where people do not follow the right way, one shall go to a place where they are just and follow the way of good folk. If all the countries that one knows or hears about follow a way that is not good—as in our time—or if because of military campaigns or plague one is unable to reach a place with good customs, then one shall dwell alone in solitude. As it said, "Let him dwell alone and be silent" (Lamentations 3:28) (*Mishneh Torah,* book 1, treatise 2, chapter 6:1)

Strive for the Middle Way

The right way is the mean in every single one of a person's character traits. It is the character trait that is equally distant from the two extremes, not close to one or the other. Therefore, the wise of olden times commanded that a person continuously appraise, evaluate, and direct one's character traits in the middle way in order to achieve perfection. . . .

One should be neither exceedingly stingy nor squander all one's wealth, but shall give charity according to his means and provide a fitting amount to the needy. One shall be neither buffoonish nor morose, but rejoice calmly with a cheerful demeanor all his days. Thus shall one order the rest of his character traits. This is the way of the wise. . . .

We are commanded to walk in these middle ways, which are the good and right ways. As it is said: "And you shall walk in His ways." Thus the sages taught in explaining this commandment: "Just as the Creator is called gracious, you too be gracious; just as the Creator is called merciful, you too be merciful. And, just as the Creator is called holy, you too be holy." (*Mishneh Torah*, book 1, treatise 2, chapter 1:4–5)

Don't Be Envious about Possessions

It is no wrong or injustice that one person has many bags of finest myrrh and garments embroidered with gold, while another has not those things, which are not necessary for our sustenance. One who has them has not thereby obtained control over anything that could be an essential addition to his being but has only obtained something illusory or deceptive.

The other person, who does not possess that which is not needed for his sustenance, does not miss anything indispensable.

This is the rule at all times and in all places. (*The Guide for the Perplexed,* book 3, chapter 12)

Don't Be Acquisitive

When the soul becomes accustomed to superfluous things, it acquires a strong habit of desiring things that are necessary for the preservation of neither the individual nor the species. This desire can be limitless. But things that are truly necessary are few in number and restricted by limitations.

What is superfluous is endless. For example, you desire to have your vessels made of silver, but golden vessels are still better. Others may even have vessels made of sapphire, or perhaps made of emeralds or rubies—or any other substance that could be suggested.

Those who are ignorant and perverse in their thought are constantly in trouble and pain because they cannot get as much of superfluous things as someone else possesses. As a rule, they expose themselves to great dangers—for example, by sea voyage or service to kings—and all of this for the purpose of obtaining that which is superfluous and unnecessary. (*The Guide for the Perplexed,* book 3, chapter 12)

The Price of a High Reputation

Your questions are very significant and I have answered them all. Unfortunately, my response was delayed owing to my prolonged illness and unfavorable times. I was laid up almost a year, and even now, although out of danger, I still have not recovered sufficiently to get out of bed completely. Compounding my physical condition, I am burdened with a multitude of patients who exhaust me and give me no respite day and night. Alas, one has to pay a price for a reputation that has spread to even neighboring countries. (Letter to Rabbi Jonathan Ha-Kohen)

Fasting for Personal Growth

Just as a community should fast when it is in trouble, so should an individual fast when in trouble. Thus, if a dear one is ill, or if one is lost in the wilderness or is confined in prison, it is his duty to fast on this account and to solicit God's mercy by reciting [prayers]. (*Mishneh Torah*, book 3, treatise 9, chapter 1:10)

———

If one forgets and eats on a fast day, he may nevertheless complete his fast. (*Mishneh Torah*, book 3, treatise 9, chapter 1:15)

———

If one is fasting—whether because he is personally in trouble or has had a bad dream or because he is participating in a communal fast observed for a communal calamity—he should not pamper himself nor act frivolously nor be joyful and glad of heart but should act seriously and mournfully. (*Mishneh Torah*, book 3, treatise 9, chapter 1:14)

Coping with a Bad Dream

If one has a bad dream, he should fast on the next day so that he might look searchingly into his conduct and repent. He should observe a fast even if the next day is a Sabbath . . . and should during each service recite the prayer beginning "Answer us, O Lord." (*Mishneh Torah*, book 3, treatise 9, chapter 1:12)

Don't Dwell on the Past

Our eyes are set in the front and not in the back. One should therefore look ahead of oneself and not behind. (*Letter to the Jews of Marseilles*)

3

All Learning Is Sacred

I T'S PERHAPS impossible to overestimate the importance
of learning for Maimonides' entire approach to human
existence. More than simply an enjoyable mental activity,
or even as a means to a worthy religious end, he regarded all
study as an exalted endeavor that actually connects us with the
divine. It would be no exaggeration to say that he regarded
the scholar—though one, of course, whose daily regimen was
rooted in ethical conduct—as the highest contributor to humanity. To some Jewish theologians, such a glorification
seemed excessive.

As a child, Moses ben Maimon was educated in Córdoba,
primarily by his father and rabbinic tutors. He showed pre-
cocity in both religious and secular subjects—by some historical accounts, even delving into his father's medical treatises
to gain additional intellectual mastery. Though forced into
weary wandering with his family for many years, he nevertheless sustained an undaunted focus—avidly studying with

leading rabbis of the day. It's hard to imagine anything that might have deterred his iron-willed dedication to scholarship.

Throughout Maimonides' multifaceted life, he also cherished the experience of serving as teacher and mentor. In Fez he eagerly taught courses in astronomy, mathematics, Greek philosophy, logic, and other secular subjects. Later, despite a huge workload while serving simultaneously as Egypt's Jewish communal leader and as full-time physician to Saladin's court, he tutored those seeking greater knowledge of Judaism. For him such work was a sacred duty for which compensation was inappropriate. In his late career he even dedicated his magnum opus, *Guide for the Perplexed,* to a prized student, Joseph ibn Aknin.

It's fascinating to see that Maimonides—as a profound thinker who wrestled with ultimate issues of faith and reason, health and illness, earthly existence and the afterlife—valued education so much that he even gave specific guidelines for class size and proper classroom behavior for pupils and teachers.

For Rabbi Moses ben Maimon, teaching is among the noblest and most sacred of professions. To honor and celebrate one's teachers is therefore an ethical responsibility for everyone. He especially stressed the importance of fostering during youth a daily routine of learning—so that study becomes a habitual and "natural" activity throughout one's life. It's an insightful prescription for our own society today.

TEACHINGS

Cultivate Wisdom

Love wisdom: "Seek her as silver and search for her as for a hidden treasure" (Proverbs 2:4). Gather in the homes of the wise who study and teach. Let their abode be your destination, for there you will derive pleasure, listening to their words of wisdom and chastisement, their new interpretations, and the subtle reasoning of their students. In your heart be zealous of the learned and despise the ignorant. (Letter on Ethics to Son, Abraham)

———

I want to posit with you this ethical principle: the faculty of study is of great value for validating truth, setting your mind at ease, and dispelling perplexity. (Letter on Ethics to Son, Abraham)

Start Learning at an Early Age

Acquire knowledge in your youth, when you are still inclined to absorb the techniques of others and when your mind is free, unmarred by fixated thoughts and a feeble memory. For there may come a time when you will want to learn but lack the ability to absorb—and even that which you will be able to acquire will have little value, for it will remain unclear. And even that which you will grasp will not be sustained but easily forgotten. (Letter on Ethics to Son, Abraham)

Motivate Your Learning

The process of learning will prove a pleasant and easy experience if you stay there willingly with the intention of deriving from your studies a higher purpose. However, if you will be distracted from your studies, the value of your stay will be wasted—for you will not learn anything and your sedentary state will be unbearable and injurious to your health. When you finally depart from the house of learning, be conscious of what you are taking home with you. Fasten it in your mind and deposit it in your heart. (Letter on Ethics to Son, Abraham)

Students and Teachers

One who has instructed another in any subject, and has improved his knowledge, may in like manner be regarded as the parent of the person taught. Thus pupils of the prophets are called "sons of the prophets." (*The Guide for the Perplexed,* book 1, chapter 7)

———

Children should be sent to school at the age of six or seven, according to their physical strength and development. But no child should be entered below the age of six. (*Mishneh Torah,* book 1, treatise 3, chapter 2:2)

———

Twenty-five children may be taught by one teacher. If there are more than twenty-five pupils but fewer than forty, an assistant should be engaged to help with the instruction. If there are more than forty, two elementary school teachers are appointed. (*Mishneh Torah,* book 1, treatise 3, chapter 2:5)

Be Sure to Read Aloud

Whoever studies aloud retains his learning, but one who reads silently forgets quickly. (*Mishneh Torah,* book 1, treatise 3, chapter 3:12)

Advice for Pupils

A student should not say "I understand" when he does not but should keep on asking questions repeatedly. (*Mishneh Torah,* book 1, treatise 3, chapter 4:4)

———

A student must not feel ashamed because his peers have grasped a subject at once, or soon after it was taught a second time, while it has taken him many times to learn it. If he were to feel embarrassment because of this, he would be attending school without learning anything. (*Mishneh Torah,* book 1, treatise 3, chapter 4:5)

_____

A teacher should not be asked any questions immediately upon entering the classroom, until he gets clearly focused. Nor should a student ask a question when he enters until he sits down and is at ease. Two students should not ask questions at the same time. The teacher should not be asked questions about a different subject but only about the subject at hand, so that he should not get embarrassed. (*Mishneh Torah,* book 1, treatise 3, chapter 4:6)

_____

When you ask or answer a question, do not speak in a rapid, confusing, shouting, or mocking tone. Rather, use choice language and articulate clearly in a subdued voice. Show a contemplative attitude, as one who seeks to learn and discover the truth, rather than being a contentious person who is anxious to prevail over his opponent. (Letter on Ethics to Son, Abraham)

_____

Where there are no teachers, a person must serve as his own teacher. (Commentary on *Pirkey Avot,* chapter 2)

Don't Be an Underachiever

Of one who neglects his studies—or who has never studied— it is said: "He has despised the word of the Lord" (Numbers

15:31). This also refers to one who fails to continue his studies even if he is a great scholar—for he thereby neglects the positive precept of advancing his learning, which is the highest commandment. (Letter to Joseph ibn Gabir)

Advice for Teachers

If a teacher has taught a subject and his students fail to understand it, he must not get agitated or angry with them but should review the lesson with them many times until they finally grasp it. (*Mishneh Torah,* book 1, treatise 3, chapter 4:4)

———

Just as pupils are required to honor their teacher, so the teacher ought to be courteous and friendly toward his pupils. The sages said: "Let the honor of your student be as your own." One should be interested in his pupils and kindly toward them, for they are the spiritual children who give pleasure in this world and in the World to Come. (*Mishneh Torah,* book 1, treatise 3, chapter 5:12)

Treasure Your Pupils

Students increase a teacher's wisdom and broaden his mind. The sages said: "I have learned much from my teachers, even more from my colleagues, but I have learned the most from my students." (*Mishneh Torah,* book 1, treatise 3, chapter 5:13)

Always Study with a Companion

One cannot compare the effect of individual study to that of study with another person. [Subject matter studied with] another person will be retained better and will be clarified more. This applies even if the other person is at one's own level of wisdom and even when he is on a lower level. (Commentary on *Pirkey Avot,* chapter 2)

Seeking Truth in Life

When I have a difficult subject before me—when I find the road narrow and can see no other way of teaching a well-established truth except by pleasing one intelligent person and displeasing ten thousand fools—I prefer to address myself to the one person and to take no notice whatever of the condemnation of the multitude. (*The Guide for the Perplexed,* introduction)

———

Once established by proof, a truth neither gains force or certainty by the consent of all the scholars nor loses it by the general dissent. (*The Guide for the Perplexed,* introduction)

———

The truth of a thing does not become greater by its frequent repetition, nor is it lessened by lack of repetition. (*Letter on Resurrection*)

———

Do not consider a thing as proof because you find it written in books. For just as a liar will deceive with his tongue, he will not be deterred from doing the same thing with his pen. Only utter fools accept a thing as convincing proof merely because it is in writing. (*Letter to Yemen*)

Truth Is Independent of Its Presenter

Since these concepts can be proven in an unshakable manner, leaving no room for question, the identity of the author—be

he prophet or a gentile—is of no concern. When the rationale
of a matter . . . has proven truthful in an unshakable manner, we
do not rely on [the personal authority] of the person who
made these statements but on the proofs that he has presented.
(*Mishneh Torah,* book 14, treatise 17, chapter 24:1)

Embracing Criticism

I am sure you realize how I labored day and night for almost
ten years to compose the *Mishneh Torah.* People of your scholarly attainments appreciate the significance of this work. I have
gathered scattered materials from a variety of sources and
attempted to arrange them into a systematized, scholarly code.

Is it any wonder then that some errors might have crept
into such a complicated study, especially at my age when one
is apt to forget certain references? For these reasons, I would
admonish every student of my work to investigate scrupu-
lously the text and check out the content and conclusions
reached. Let no one feel restrained from examining critically
every detail of the book. . . . You have rendered me a great
service with your critical observations, and by the same token,
I shall appreciate the efforts of anyone who will emulate your
example and point out any error he may find in the book.
(Letter to Rabbi Jonathan Ha-Kohen)

Translating Effectively

The translator who proposes to render each word literally and
adheres slavishly to the order of the words and sentences in the
original will meet much difficulty, and the results will be
doubtful and corrupt. This is not the right way. [Rather,] the
translator should first try to grasp the sense of the subject thoroughly and then state the theme with perfect clarity in the
other language. This, however, cannot be done without chang-

ing the order of the words, using many words for one word or vice versa, and adding or taking away words, so that the subject may be perfectly intelligible in the language in which he translates. (Letter to Samuel ibn Tibbon)

The Ancient Philosophers

The works of Aristotle are the basis for all of those philosophical books. While the works of Plato, the teacher of Aristotle, are profound and substantive, one may apprehend their essential notions in other works, especially those of Aristotle, whose writings embrace all philosophical concepts developed previously. For Aristotle reached the highest level of knowledge to which humanity can ascend, with the exception of one who experiences the emanation of the Divine Spirit—who can attain the level of prophecy—above which there is no higher stage. (Letter to Samuel ibn Tibbon)

Literary Form and Content

Poems, no matter in what language, must be examined as to substance. I have heard some of our old and pious scholars at weddings and at other feasts protest sharply against the singing of an Arabic song, even if it was in praise of bravery or generosity, or in praise of wine. But when the singer intoned a Hebrew song of forbidden and ugly poetry, they did not object.

This is rather an unwise attitude. A word is not forbidden or permitted, esteemed or despised, or commanded to be spoken because of the language in which it is expressed but because of its meaning. If the content is right, it may be put in any language whatsoever; if the text of the song is vulgar, then it is forbidden, irrespective of its language. And I should like to add this: If there are two poems of a similar displeasing content, one in Hebrew and the other in Arabic or Persian, it is far more detestable to listen to the Hebrew recitation, because the standard of Hebrew demands that it be used for valued matters only. (Commentary on *Pirkey Avot*, chapter 1)

————

All of my compositions are to the point and brief. I do not seek to enlarge the size of the books nor to lose time on what yields no benefit. (*Letter on Resurrection*)

————

It makes no difference whether one pursues his studies in Hebrew, Arabic, or Aramaic, as long as one understands the issues involved. This applies especially to the commentaries and the summaries. The most important thing is to be involved in learning. (Letter to Joseph ibn Gabir)

When a Scholar Dies

The day when news of the death of a scholar is received is regarded as though one were in his presence, and lamentation is made for him—though the place of burial is distant. (*Mishneh Torah*, book 14, treatise 4, chapter 11:5)

Mourning a Sage

Whoever fails to mourn for a sage will not live long, and whoever fails to mourn for a worthy person deserves to be buried alive. Whoever sheds tears for a worthy person, the Holy One, blessed be He, has a reward in store for him. (*Mishneh Torah*, book 14, treatise 4, chapter 12:2)

4

SPIRITUAL AWAKENING
AND PROPHECY

BASIC TO Maimonides' vast legacy has been his emphasis on prophetic consciousness. Far more than other rabbinic thinkers of his time, he emphasized that this exalted state of awareness is not only *natural* to human capability but *attainable* by nearly everyone who cultivates spiritual growth in daily life. In this sense, Maimonides had a truly universalist and "democratic" viewpoint—one that encouraged individuals everywhere to develop their higher sensitivities through conscious effort and attention. For he believed that each of us, regardless of family background or status, has a tremendous unused potential for spiritual achievement.

Certainly as a practicing physician, Maimonides was intimately acquainted with emotional turmoil, unrest, and illness. Both his Judaic and his medical writings are filled with references to the "dark side" of human nature and such negative states as anger, sadness, and worry. He strongly believed that, when chronic, these emotions serve as serious blockages to inner development. Yet in Maimonides' influential view, we can diligently learn to overcome these tendencies and thereby connect more fully with the divine that surrounds us.

In this regard, was Maimonides a kabbalist—perhaps teaching chosen disciples secretly—as some commentators have long insisted? The answer is unequivocally no. Though later, renowned Jewish mystics like Abraham Abulafia of Spain eagerly cited his writings—especially *Guide for the Perplexed*—it's likely that Maimonides would have sternly disapproved. His works contain no references to central kabbalistic concepts like the ten *sefirot* (divine emanations) and the Tree of Life. Nor did he cite texts in which such ideas appeared. Temperamentally, too, he was always more comfortable with measured rationalistic discourse than with the poetic and imaginative exuberance of full-blown mysticism. He wrote with disdain about what scholars today call "practical Kabbalah"—associated with amulets, astrology, and divinatory techniques.

Nevertheless, Maimonides' approach to prophetic consciousness has for centuries held an undeniable fascination for kabbalists—and exerted an encouraging influence on Jewish mystical study. For he clearly taught that personal revelation is not only possible in the postbiblical world but within our reach through the right daily regimen. And, in this powerful regard, he kept Judaism's door open for ecstatic seekers and visionaries to the present day.

TEACHINGS

Spiritual Slumber

If we desire to attain human perfection—and to be truly people of God—we must awaken from our sleep. (*The Guide for the Perplexed,* book 3, chapter 52)

Higher Consciousness

At times, revelation shines so brilliantly that we perceive it as clear as day. [But] then our nature and habit draw a veil over our perception, and we return to a darkness almost as dense as before. We are like those who, though beholding frequent flashes of lightning, still find themselves amid the thickest darkness of the night.

For some persons, the lightning flashes in rapid succession, and they seem to be bathed in continuous light. Their night is as clear as day. This was the degree of prophetic excellence attained by Moses, the greatest of prophets. Some perceive the prophetic flash at long intervals; this is the degree of most prophets. For others, only once during the whole night is a flash of lightning perceived. This is the case with those of whom we are informed, "They prophesied, and [then] they did no more" (Numbers 11:25). (*The Guide for the Perplexed,* introduction)

Experiencing the Divine

I have shown you that the radiance that emanates from God onto us is the link that joins us to God. It is within your power to strengthen that bond if you so choose—or to weaken it gradually until it breaks, if you prefer that. It will only become strong when you employ it in the love of God and seek that love. It will be weakened when you direct your thoughts to other things. (*The Guide for the Perplexed,* book 3, chapter 51)

———

You must know that even if you were the wisest person with respect to the true knowledge of God, you break the bond between yourself and God whenever you turn your thoughts entirely to necessary food or any necessary business. For then

you are not with God, and He is not with you—your relationship is actually interrupted in those moments.

The pious were therefore particular in restricting the times
in which they could not meditate upon the name of God and
cautioned others about it, saying, "Let not your minds be vacant
from reflections upon God." (*The Guide for the Perplexed,* book
3, chapter 51)

Encountering the Divine

Those who have no knowledge of God are like those who are
in constant darkness and have never seen light. We have explained in this sense the biblical verse "The wicked shall be
silent in darkness" (1 Samuel, 2:9), whereas those who possess
that knowledge and direct their thoughts constantly toward it
are, as it were, always in bright sunshine. Those who have the
knowledge of God but who are at times engaged by other
themes experience, as it were, a cloudy day—the sun does not
shine for them on account of the cloud that intervenes between them and God. (*The Guide for the Perplexed,* book 2,
chapter 51)

Boundaries of the Human Mind

It was not the object of the prophets and the sages in their utterances to close the gates of investigation entirely and to prevent the [human] mind from comprehending what is within its
reach. [Rather], their whole object was to declare that there is a
limit to human reason—where it must halt. (*The Guide for the
Perplexed,* book 1, chapter 32)

The Nature of Prophecy

The prophets sometimes prophesy in allegories. They use a
term allegorically, and in the same prophecy the meaning of

the allegory is given. In our dreams, we sometimes believe that we are awake and relate a dream to another person who explains the dream—all of this goes on while we dream.

Our sages call this "a dream interpreted in a dream." In other cases, we learn the meaning of the dream after waking from sleep. The same is true with prophetic allegories. Some are interpreted in the prophetic vision [itself].

There are other prophetic allegories whose meaning is not given in a prophetic vision. The prophet learns it when he awakens from his sleep. (*The Guide for the Perplexed,* book 2, chapter 43)

The Two Forms of Prophecy

Prophecy is given either in a vision or in a dream—as we have said many times. (*The Guide for the Perplexed,* book 2, chapter 44)

Prophecy and Imagery

It is undoubtedly clear and evident that most prophecies are given in images, for this is the characteristic of the imaginative faculty: the organ of prophecy. (*The Guide for the Perplexed,* book 2, chapter 47)

Barriers to Higher Experience

The corporeal element of man is a large screen and partition that prevents him from perfectly perceiving abstract ideals. This would be the case even if the corporeal element were as pure and superior as the substance of the spheres. How much more must this be the case with our dark and opaque body! However great the exertion of our mind may be to comprehend the Divine Being, or any of the ideals, we find a screen and a partition between Him and ourselves. (*The Guide for the Perplexed,* book 3, chapter 9)

———

The prophets frequently hint at the existence of a partition between God and us. They say He is concealed from us in vapors, in darkness, in mist, or in a thick cloud, or use similar figures to express that on account of our bodies we are unable to comprehend His essence. That is the meaning of the words "Clouds and darkness are round about Him" (Psalm 97:2). The prophets tell us that the difficulty consists in the grossness of our substance. (*The Guide for the Perplexed,* book 3, chapter 9)

Features of Prophecy

The prophet may perceive that which he hears with the greatest possible intensity, just as a person may hear thunder in his dream or perceive a storm or an earthquake. Such dreams are frequent. The prophet may also hear the prophecy in ordinary common speech, without anything unusual. For example, take the account of the prophet Samuel. When he was called in a prophetic vision, he believed that the priest Eli called him— and this happened three times consecutively. . . . Samuel did not yet know the Lord, and it had not been revealed to him that the word of God is communicated in this way. (*The Guide for the Perplexed,* book 2, chapter 43)

Traits of Prophets

Just as not all who have a true dream are prophets, so it cannot be said of everyone who is assisted in a certain undertaking— as in the acquisition of property or some other personal advantage—that the spirit of the Lord came upon him or that the Lord was with him or that he performed his actions by the Holy Spirit.

We apply such phrases only to those who have accomplished something very good and grand or something that leads to that end—for example, the success of Joseph in the house of the Egyptian, which was the first cause evidently leading to great events that occurred subsequently. (*The Guide for the Perplexed,* book 2, chapter 44)

The Nature of Prophecy

Prophecy is, in truth and reality, an emanation sent forth by God through the medium of the Active Intellect: first to one's rational faculty and then to one's imaginative faculty. It is the highest degree and greatest perfection humans can attain. It consists in the most perfect development of the imaginative faculty. (*The Guide for the Perplexed,* book 2, chapter 36)

———

Prophecy is a faculty that cannot in any way be found in a person—or acquired through a culture of one's mental and moral faculties, even if these were as good and perfect as possible—unless combined with the highest natural excellence of the imaginative faculty. (*The Guide for the Perplexed,* book 2, chapter 36)

The Purpose of Imagination

[Now], part of the function of the imaginative faculty is, as you well know, to retain sensory impressions, to combine them, and chiefly to form images. But the principal and highest function is performed when our senses are at rest and pause in their action, for then the highest function receives—to some extent—divine inspiration in the measure as it is predisposed for this influence. This is the nature of those dreams which prove true, and also of prophecy, the difference being one of quantity, not quality.

Thus, our sages say that dream is the sixtieth part of prophecy, and no comparison could be made between two things of different kinds. For we cannot say the perfection of the human individual is so many times the perfection of a horse. In this regard, the Talmud aptly comments: "Dream is the unripe fruit of prophecy" [*Bereshit Rabba,* section 17].

This is an excellent comparison, for the unripe fruit is really the fruit to some extent—only it has fallen from the tree before it was fully developed and ripe. In a similar manner, the action of our imaginative faculty during sleep is the same as at the time when it receives a prophecy, only in the first case it is not fully developed and has not yet reached its highest degree. (*The Guide for the Perplexed,* book 2, chapter 36)

Personality and Prophecy

Do not be surprised to learn that a few moral imperfections lessen the degree of prophetic inspiration. In fact, we find that some moral vices cause prophecy to be entirely withdrawn. Thus, for instance, anger may do this, as our rabbis say: "If a prophet becomes enraged, the spirit of prophecy departs from him."

Grief and anxiety may also cause a cessation of prophecy, as in the case of the patriarch Jacob, who, during the days when he mourned for his son Joseph, was deprived of the Holy Spirit, until he received the news that Joseph was alive.

The sages say, moreover, that "the spirit of prophecy rests

not upon the idle, nor upon the sad, but upon the joyous."
(*Eight Chapters,* chapter 7)

———

Whoever gives way to anger, if a wise person, one's wisdom
departs, and if a prophet, one's prophecy departs as well. (*Mishneh Torah,* book 4, treatise 2, chapter 2:3)

How to Make Use of Solitude

When you are by yourself—as in awakening from sleep—be
careful to meditate in such precious moments on nothing but
the contemplative worship of God: that is, to approach God
and to minister before God in the true manner that I have
described to you—not with hollow emotions.

This conduct I consider to be the highest perfection wise
persons can attain by proper training. (*The Guide for the Perplexed,* book 3, chapter 51)

Removing Barriers to the Divine

Let us pray to God and beseech Him to clear and remove from
our way everything that forms an obstruction and a partition
between us and Him—although most of these obstacles are
our creation. As the prophet Isaiah declared, "Your iniquities
have separated you from your God" (Isaiah 59:2). (*The Guide
for the Perplexed,* book 3, chapter 51)

———

It is clear that we ourselves are the cause of this hiding of the
[divine] face—and the screen that separates us from God is of
our own creation. (*The Guide for the Perplexed,* book 3, chapter 51)

Prophecy versus Philosophy

You should know that there is one form of cognition superior to philosophy, and that is prophecy. It operates in a different sphere and requires no proofs and no arguments. Once it is determined that a conclusion is the result of prophetic processes, no other authentication is necessary. This was the case with every prophet—who had to validate only his identity as a prophet and not the content of his prophecy. Transcending natural phenomena, prophecy, unlike other forms of knowledge, is superior to any natural proofs. (Letter to Hasdai Ha-Levi)

5

SOCIAL RELATIONS
AND LEADERSHIP

IN MANY WAYS, Maimonides was the quintessential scholar—who even as a youth preferred solitary cerebral activities like erudite reading and writing. By his early twenties he had already produced original treatises on such abstruse topics as the intricacies of the Jewish calendar and the terminology of ancient Greek logic. Despite the hardships of forced exile for years throughout hostile Muslim Spain, he was able to sustain brilliant rabbinic scholarship.

Yet Maimonides was also a man with keen understanding of human relations—what today psychologists call social intelligence. Indeed, it's a vital aspect of his influential life that's curiously—and strikingly—overlooked by most biographers and historians even today. For not only was Rabbi Moses ben Maimon appointed leader of Egypt's Jewish community at a young age, he also conducted this important administrative position well and navigated effectively through its inevitable political shoals. Much admired for such achievement, he was later reappointed to this prominent post and eventually became revered as the foremost Jewish leader of his time.

Acting simultaneously as *nagid* and court physician to Saladin, Maimonides from all accounts likewise served with great social competence. Not only was his personal integrity unimpeachable but also as an alien Jew he successfully gained the confidence and eventual friendship of those wielding great power in the Muslim world. Such attainment bespeaks a true mastery of social relationships that can hardly be attributed merely to scholarly talent.

Indeed, Maimonides' writings offer considerable advice on sociability and leadership. It's therefore clear that he recognized this important dimension of human life—and viewed its success as depending on specific personality traits. Thus, widely interspersed throughout his Judaic, philosophical, and medical treatises are specific tips for relating well with others, becoming a leader, and acting in ways consistent with such a position.

As is true of Maimonides' other perspectives on individual achievement, he viewed leadership as essentially learned rather than inborn—involving the cultivation of certain specific personality traits such as cheerfulness, altruism, and honesty. It also required a desire to nurture caring relations with others. Similar to the processes involved in acquiring the wisdom of a sage and even the lofty consciousness of a prophet, the threefold qualities of motivation, self-discipline, and daily practice were paramount.

TEACHINGS

Honor Your Teachers

Just we are commanded to honor and revere our parents, so it is our duty to honor and revere our teachers. For our parents have secured for us life in this world, but our teachers who have taught us wisdom secure for us life in the World to Come. (*Mishneh Torah,* book 1, treatise 3, chapter 5:1)

———

There is no honor higher than that which is due to our teachers, no reverence more profound than that which should be bestowed on them. The sages said: "The reverence for your teacher should be like the reverence for heaven." (*Mishneh Torah,* book 1, treatise 3, chapter 5:1)

Taking the Initiative

Act with self-assertiveness and self-respect. (Letter on Ethics to Son, Abraham)

Choose the Right Companions

Avoid the company of the foolish and the street idlers, and juvenile games from which emanate only evil. Select always the company of the great and the wise, but behave in their presence with humility and in a subdued manner.

Exert your mental faculties and open the "ears" of your heart to hear and comprehend their words. Consider carefully what they reject or accept, weigh probingly one argument against another. Then you will be wise.

Guard your tongue from entreating them unduly. Condense your remarks into one sentence, keeping in mind that abundance of speech increases error. Never appear impudent or insolent before them, but at the same time, do not be embarrassed to ask questions as long as it is done at the right time and in suitable language. (Letter on Ethics to Son, Abraham)

Watch Your Words

Weigh every word before uttering it, for once articulated, it cannot be withdrawn. (Letter on Ethics to Son, Abraham)

Appearing to Be Angry

Should a person desire to impress fear upon one's children, household, or community—if their leader—and wish to display anger that they return to good behavior, one may show oneself in their presence as though angry for the purpose of reproving them but ought nevertheless to be composed within, like one who pretends to be vexed but is really not. (*Mishneh Torah,* book 4, treatise 2, chapter 3:3)

Always Be Trustworthy

It was my trustworthiness that led me into places where my kinfolk could never have brought me and bestowed upon me an inheritance greater than that of my parents. It invested me with authority over those greater and better than myself, so that I prospered and became useful to myself and others.

Therefore be zealous about the welfare of others, even beyond the call of duty. Keep your word and do not discredit the evidence of public or private promises, whether made by a note or symbolic act, or to a witness. (Letter on Ethics to Son, Abraham)

———

Reject and repudiate fraudulent, sly, underhanded, or illegal practices. Woe unto one who builds his edifice on such dealings. He will be abandoned in the prime of his life, and his end will be disgraceful. (Letter on Ethics to Son, Abraham)

———

To maintain my intellectual and ethical integrity is far more important than to prevail with insults over the foolhardy. (Letter to Joseph ibn Aknin)

Avoid Getting Drawn into Disputes

Remain aloof and stay at a distance from quarreling relatives, lest you suffer from their contentiousness. (Letter on Ethics to Son, Abraham)

Cultivate Patience

Extol the quality of patience. For in it lies genuine strength and true triumph. The example of your patience will help to improve decent people and prevail over the wicked by your refusal to imitate them. (Letter on Ethics to Son, Abraham)

———

Judges should be patient in coming to a decision and should not hastily issue a ruling without contemplating it in depth. For it is possible that later they will realize concepts that were not apparent to them in their original conception of the matter. (Commentary on *Pirkey Avot*, chapter 1)

Your Appearance Matters

Dress in accordance with your means. (Letter on Ethics to Son, Abraham)

———

The king of the Jews [must have] his hair trimmed every day, pay due regard to his personal appearance, and adorn himself with beautiful clothes. (*Mishneh Torah*, book 14, treatise 5, chapter 2:5)

How Judges Must Behave

The Divine Presence dwells in the midst of any competent Jewish tribunal. Therefore it behooves the judges to sit in court enwrapped [in fringed robes], in a state of fear and reverence, and in a serious frame of mind. They are forbidden to behave frivolously, jest, or engage in idle talk. They should concentrate their minds on matters of Torah and wisdom. (*Mishneh Torah,* book 14, treatise 1, chapter 3:7)

Bestowing Dignity on Others

A leader is also forbidden to treat the people with disrespect, though they be ignorant. He should not force his way through congregants [to get to his seat], for though they be uninformed and lowly, they are the children of Abraham, Isaac, and Jacob, of the hosts of God, brought forth out of Egypt with great power and a mighty hand. (*Mishneh Torah,* book 14, treatise 1, chapter 25:2)

The Conduct of a Leader

As soon as one is appointed leader of the community, he is forbidden to eat, drink, and get intoxicated in the presence of many, or attend assemblies of ignorant people or social parties. Woe onto those judges who make a practice of such indulgences, for [their] contempt of the Torah of Moses. They despise its judgments, lower its standards, bring it down to the dust, and cause evil to themselves and their children's children in this world and the world to come. (*Mishneh Torah,* book 14, treatise 2, chapter 25:4)

Maintain Your Dignity

It is forbidden to see the king [of the Jews] when he is naked or when his hair is being cut or when he is taking a bath or when he dries himself. (*Mishneh Torah,* book 14, treatise 5, chapter 2:3)

Lead with Humility

Just as Scripture accords great honor to the king [of the Jews] and bids all to pay him honor, so it bids him to cultivate a humble and lowly spirit, as it is written: "And my heart is humbled within me" (Psalms 109:22). He must not exercise his authority in a supercilious manner. . . . He should deal graciously and compassionately with the small and the great, conduct their affairs in their best interests, be wary of the honor of even the lowliest. When he addresses the public collectively, he should use gentle language, as did David when he said: "Hear me, my brethren, and my people" (I Chronicles 28:2). (*Mishneh Torah,* book 14, treatise 5, chapter 2:6)

It is forbidden to lead the community in a domineering and arrogant manner. One should exercise one's authority in a spirit of humility and reverence. The man at the head of the congregation who arouses excessive fear in the hearts of the members for any but a religious purpose will therefore be punished. (*Mishneh Torah,* book 14, treatise 1, chapter 25:1)

If a person's identity is unknown and his conduct could be interpreted as either good or evil, it is an obligation [for those who follow the path of piety] to judge him in a favorable manner. (Commentary on *Pirkey Avot,* chapter 1)

One of the ways of detecting a wise person is to see whether he speaks with measured words, as it is said in the Mishnah

(3:13): "Silence is a fence for wisdom." (Commentary on *Pirkey Avot,* chapter 1)

Communicating with Others

A person's instructions reflect his character, and good people do not instruct people to do bad things, but warn against them. (Commentary on *Pirkey Avot,* chapter 5)

———

The following narrative is told about Aaron. When he would feel or hear that a person has wickedness within him or that he would commit sins, he would [always] greet him first, become friendly with him, and speak with him frequently.

This would cause the other person to become embarrassed and say, "Woe is me. If Aaron knew my inner thoughts or were aware of my deeds, he would not let himself see me; how much more so would he not speak to me. Surely he considers me to be pious. I will make his conception true and repent and become one of his students again." (Commentary on *Pirkey Avot,* chapter 2)

Work with Dedication

One should know that before communicating ideas to the general public, it is essential to review these thoroughly two, three, or four times in private prior to exposing them [orally] in public. Our sages derived such a procedure from the saying (Job 28:37), "Then he saw it and declared it, he established it and searched it out." However, when one is involved in putting something into writing, an even greater effort of a possible thousand-fold review is required. (*Letter on Martyrdom*)

Every Person Matters

Surely every person has the potential to cause damage or to promote good, even with regard to things of minor concern and little value. If you have disgraced a person, he may cause you harm. (Commentary on *Pirkey Avot*, chapter 4)

Always Have Friends

It is well known that one requires friends all of his lifetime. When one is in good health and prosperous, he enjoys the company of his friends. In time of trouble, he is in need of them. In old age, when his body is weak, he is assisted by them. (*The Guide for the Perplexed*, book 3, chapter 49)

———

A person should always have a friend who will [help him] better all aspects of his conduct, as our sages commented, "Either companionship or death." If one does not find a friend easily, one must make efforts in this direction. If necessary, one should procure his friendship until [true] friendship is established. One should not cease accommodating oneself to the other person's nature until such friendship has been established. Thus, the ethical masters have taught, "Do not establish friendship according to your nature; establish friendship according to your friend's nature."

When each of the friends conducts himself according to this directive, the desire of each one will be to fulfill the will of his colleague. Thus they will both share a single goal. How appropriate is the statement of Aristotle, "Your other friend is really yourself." (Commentary on *Pirkey Avot*, chapter 1)

———

In general there are three types of friends: a friend befriended for the sake of benefit, a friend befriended for the sake of satisfaction, and a friend befriended for the sake of a higher purpose.

Examples of friends befriended for the sake of benefit are two partners, or the relationship between a king and his army.

There are two types of friends befriended for the sake of satisfaction: a friend whom one trusts and a friend who grants one pleasure. An example of a friend who grants one pleasure is the relationship between men and women during marriage.

A friend whom one trusts refers to a person on whom one can rely without withholding anything from him, neither deed nor word. He reveals to him all of his matters—both good and bad—without worrying that shame will result either in private or in public. When a person is able to trust a colleague so thoroughly, he will derive tremendous satisfaction from talking to him and sharing his company.

A friend befriended for the sake of a higher purpose refers to a situation where both desire and focus on a single objective: doing good. Each will desire to draw strength from his colleague and to attain the good for them both. This is the type of friend the Mishnah commands us to acquire: for example, the comradeship between a teacher and his disciple and between a disciple and his teacher. (Commentary on *Pirkey Avot,* chapter 1)

When Not to Show Honor

It is forbidden to rise before a judge who has paid money to be appointed. The sages tell us to look upon him with utter contempt. (*Mishneh Torah,* book 14, treatise 1, chapter 3:9)

Judges Must Be Impartial

A judge must not conduct legal proceedings for his own friend, even if the latter has not been his best friend nor one to whom he has been intimately attached. Neither should he act as judge for one whom he dislikes, even though he is not his avowed enemy nor one who means to injure him.

It is necessary that both parties to a lawsuit should be equal in the eyes and the minds of the judges. The judge who fails to know either litigant and his activities is most likely to be a rightful judge. (*Mishneh Torah*, book 14, treatise 1, chapter 23:6)

Judicial Mind-Set

A judge should ever regard himself as if a sword were placed upon his neck, with Gehenna [the Underworld] gaping under him. He should know whom he is judging, before whom he is judging, and who will punish him for deviating from the line of truth, as it is written in Psalms (82:1): "God stands in the divine assembly, in the midst of the judges." (*Mishneh Torah*, book 14, treatise 1, chapter 23:8)

Fairness Is Paramount

Two scholars who dislike each other must not act as judges together, since this might result in perverted justice. Owing to the hostility between them, each will be inclined to refute the other. (*Mishneh Torah*, book 14, treatise 1, chapter 23:7)

Preparation for Speaking

No one has the right to speak in public before he has rehearsed what he wants to say two, three, and four times and learned it:

then he may speak. This is what the rabbis taught. (*Letter on Martyrdom*)

Behaviors to Avoid

When a learned man behaves disgustingly in matters of trade or negotiation or receives people sullenly and insolently or is of an unfriendly disposition or has relations with others that are not founded on respect and mutual regard, he has profaned God's name. (*Letter on Martyrdom*)

Essential Qualities of Leadership

A disciple of the wise shall not shout and scream when speaking, like cattle and wild beasts. One shall not raise his voice much, but speak calmly with all one's fellow creatures. Yet one shall be careful not to be aloof—lest one's words resemble the words of the arrogant.

One greets all immediately, so that they will be pleasantly disposed toward him. One judges every person in a favorable light. One speaks in praise of others, never disparagingly. One loves peace and seeks peace

If he sees a place where his words would be useful and listened to, he speaks, and if not, he remains silent. . . .

The general rule is that one is to be among the oppressed and not the oppressors, among the insulted and not those who insult. (*Mishneh Torah,* book 1, treatise 2, chapter 5:7, 13)

6

THE WAY OF HEALTH AND LONGEVITY

MAIMONIDES' approach to wellness was vast and comprehensive, but he was a lucid writer who sought to make his suggestions both comprehensible and simple to carry out. Indeed, some of the remarks that are most applicable today can be found in a "how-to" manual he wrote for a dissolute young prince in the sultan's court. For ironically, millions of people today have acquired the kind of harmful lifestyle that in the past only figures of royalty were able to adopt.

In this fascinating work, often known as *The Preservation of Youth,* Maimonides late in life presented his outlook on achieving health and longevity. Apparently the prince was troubled by a host of disorders—ranging from depression to digestive problems—and Maimonides felt obliged to recommend both specific and general steps to well-being. Throughout this manual and others by him, three principles emerge—related to nutrition, physical exercise, and mental attitude.

Maimonides emphasized the importance of eating whole grains as the foundation of a sound diet. He explicitly warned the young prince to avoid consuming refined flour. Not surprisingly, Rabbi Moses ben Maimon likewise advised that he avoid meat and a dairy-rich diet. Believing that certain foods should not be eaten in combination, he specified in detail which should be mixed together and which eaten separately. Maimonides was unstinting in his condemnation of gluttony as a chief cause of illness. Certainly in American society today—when the average adult man or woman is considerably overweight—this viewpoint is much needed.

Criticizing the prince's sedentary lifestyle, Maimonides repeatedly advocated daily vigorous exercise. He identified certain forms of bathing as helpful, too, especially when recovering from illness. Without day-to-day exercise, he insisted, the human body systematically loses its ability to cope with the rigors of life.

Absolutely central to Maimonides' approach to wellness was his emphasis on what might be aptly called "right attitude." He stressed that our emotions play a vital role in affecting our physical well-being—and identified chronic anger, worry, and sadness as particularly destructive. In this light, he suggested that periodic soul-searching and inward "stocktaking" are crucial elements of proper health maintenance. Often our ethical conduct—the way we treat those around us—is an important indicator of our true health, he believed. Indeed, he regarded people who act in habitually unethical ways as suffering from an inner "sickness" that requires serious diagnosis and healing.

Maimonides insisted that inner balance is the key and therefore valued meditation as a useful tool. Likewise, following ancient Hebraic teachings, he highlighted the importance of adopting a cheerful demeanor toward others and of developing an attitude of gratitude for the small daily blessings in our lives. He emphasized that "when one possesses a good body and normal sensual drives that do not overwhelm him, he has truly a divine gift."

The basis of Maimonides' entire lifework and mission was that our physical, emotional, and spiritual aspects can work together in great harmony—if we desire to make that happen.

TEACHINGS

Our Divine Body

The well-being of the soul can be obtained only after that of the body has been secured. (*The Guide for the Perplexed,* book 3, chapter 27)

———

Know that the perfection of the body precedes the perfection of the soul and is like the key that opens the inner chamber. Let then the chief aim of your discipline be the perfecting of your body and the correcting of your morals, to open before you the gates of heaven. (Letter on Ethics to Son, Abraham)

———

It is impossible for one to understand God, or have any knowledge of the Creator, when he is in a poor physical condition. Consequently, it is necessary that he should keep aloof from those things that are injurious to the body and accustom himself to the use of things that are healthful and invigorating. (*Mishneh Torah,* book 1, treatise 2, chapter 4:1)

———

When one possesses a good body and normal sensual drives that do not overwhelm him, he has truly a divine gift. (Letter on Ethics to Son, Abraham)

Healthy and Sick Souls

It is a well-known assertion of philosophers that the soul can be healthy or diseased, just as the body is either healthy or diseased. These illnesses of the soul and their health to which philosophers allude undoubtedly refer to the opinions and morals of people. Therefore, I consider untrue opinions and bad morals, with all of their different varieties, as types of human illness. (*Medical Aphorisms of Moses*, book 2, chapter 25:59)

———

Vice is a disease of the soul, while virtue is a manifestation of the soul's healthy state. The ancients believed that the soul, like the body, is subject to good health and illness. The soul's healthful state is due to its condition, and that of its faculties, by which it constantly does what is right and performs what is proper, while the illness of the soul is occasioned by its condition, and that of its faculties, which results in its constantly doing wrong and performing actions that are improper. (*Eight Chapters,* chapter 3)

———

Among illnesses of the human soul, there is one that is so common that I think no one can escape—except a rare individual—even over a long period of time. This disease can be greater or lesser [in severity] just like other physical and spiritual illnesses. It consists of the fact that every person considers himself more perfect than he really is and desires and lusts that all that enters his mind should be perfect without effort and fatigue.

Among those with this condition, one finds people who are otherwise clever and wise, have already learned a philosophical or theoretical science or one of the traditional sciences, and have become proficient in that science. Such a person then gives opinions not only in the science he has mastered but also in other sciences concerning which he knows nothing at all or in which his knowledge is deficient. He speaks [with the same authority] in these sciences as in his discourses in the sciences in which he is proficient. . . . He does not want it to be said that there is something he doesn't know. (*Medical Aphorisms of Moses,* book 2, chapter 25:59)

———

The burning desire for money, craving for material pleasure, and an unfriendly approach are sicknesses caused by depression. These cause a person to despise seeing others and to hate them, preferring solitude and desolate places. This will surely bring a person to ruin. (Commentary on *Pirkey Avot,* chapter 2)

Our Emotions Affect Us

Emotions of the soul affect the body and produce great, significant, and wide-ranging changes in the state of health. Physicians must therefore advise that the emotions of the soul be watched, regularly examined, and kept well balanced. (*The Preservation of Youth,* chapter 3)

———

The reactions of all of those with hope and who anticipate security and calm are well known, as are also the various reactions in the thoughts of those who are desperate or successful. Occasionally the person who is desperate, and progresses from sadness to a feeling of misfortune, cannot see ahead because of weakness and the turbulence of his foresight. But one who is successful increases the light in his eyes exceedingly, so that it seems that even the light around him increases and grows. This is sufficiently clear and needs no elaboration. (*The Preservation of Youth,* chapter 3)

Learn to Meditate

Meditation offers much help [in self-healing], as it decreases evil thoughts, sadness, and woes. (*The Preservation of Youth,* chapter 3)

Eating and Nutrition

One should never eat except when hungry nor drink except when thirsty. One should not keep on eating until his stomach is filled but leave about a fourth part of his appetite unsatisfied. . . .

Do not eat until you have walked before the meal a sufficient distance to begin feeling warm or have done some kind of work or have undergone another form of exertion. . . .

Excessive eating is to the body of a man like deadly poison and is the root of all diseases. Most illnesses that befall men arise either from bad food or from immoderate indulgence of food, even of the wholesome kind. (Letter on Ethics to Son, Abraham)

———

Eat only to live, and ban luxurious foods. Think not that overindulging in food and drink strengthens the body and sharpens the mind—like a sack that becomes more complete the more you stuff into it.

With human beings, the opposite is true. The less one eats, the more beneficial—endowing strength to the body and clarity to the mind. (Letter on Ethics to Son, Abraham)

———

Be careful not to partake of another meal before the previous one lodged in your stomach has been properly digested. For such a practice is damaging to the body and the purse and is the source of most illness.

You may engage in strenuous work before your meal, but relax after eating. Do not eat in haste like a glutton nor stuff your mouth and swallow in one gulp. Abhor harmful foods as one loathes an enemy who has murderous intentions. (Letter on Ethics to Son, Abraham)

———

Eat less than your means—only to keep body and soul together. (Letter on Ethics to Son, Abraham)

———

After it is sifted in the sieve, the sourness-producing parts of flour should be made visible. . . . Bread should be made of rough grain, unchafed and unpolished. (*The Preservation of Youth*, chapter 1)

Building Strength

You know that the full development of any bodily faculty . . . depends on the condition of the organ by means of which that faculty acts. This organ must be the best possible regarding the organ's quality and size, and also regarding its purity of substance. Any defect in this respect cannot in any way be supplied or remedied by training. For when any organ is defective in its temperament, proper training in the best case can restore a healthy condition to some extent but cannot make the organ perfect. (*The Guide for the Perplexed*, book 2, chapter 36)

———

Day-to-day exercise is the main principle of keeping one's health and in the repulsion of most illnesses. (*The Preservation of Youth,* chapter 1)

Change Your Habits Slowly

Habit and regularity are great principles for keeping well and recovering from illness. It is not proper to change one's habits in health at once: neither in food and drink, nor in sexual activity, bath, or exercise. You should stick to your habits. And even if your habit is in contradiction to medical law, you must not separate from it but adjust to the law gradually and over a prolonged time—so that the change will not be felt.

A person must never change his habit all of a sudden, or sickness is bound to result. (*The Preservation of Youth,* chapter 4)

Right Attitude and Well-Being

There are indeed times when the agreeable may be used from a curative viewpoint. For example, when one suffers from loss of appetite, it may be stirred up by highly seasoned delicacies and tasty, palatable food. Similarly, one who suffers from sadness may rid himself of it by listening to singing and all kinds of instrumental music, by strolling through beautiful gardens and splendid buildings, by gazing upon beautiful pictures, and by doing other things that enliven the mind and dissipate gloomy moods.

Our rabbis of blessed memory say, "It is becoming that a sage should have a pleasant dwelling, a beautiful spouse, and domestic comfort, for one becomes weary, and one's mind is dulled, by continuous mental concentration upon difficult problems."

Just as the body becomes exhausted from hard labor, and then by rest and refreshment recovers, so it is necessary for the mind to have relaxation by gazing upon pictures and other beautiful objects, that its weariness may be dispelled. (*Eight Chapters,* chapter 5)

———

Picture yourself living in Noah's Ark, and you will always be at ease. (Letter on Ethics to Son, Abraham)

Under the Influence of Alcohol

In Jewish law, a purchase or sale by a drunken man, and his gifts, are valid. If, however, he has reached the condition of Lot, being too drunk to know what he is doing, his transactions mean nothing, since he has the legal status of a youngster less than six years old. (*Mishneh Torah,* book 12, treatise 1, chapter 29:18)

Happiness and Well-Being

In order to strengthen the patient's vital powers, one should employ musical instruments and tell patients happy stories that make the heart swell, narratives that will distract the mind and cause patients and their friends to laugh. One should select as attendants and caretakers those who can cheer up the patient. This is a must in every illness. In the absence of a physician, one must figure it out for himself. (*The Preservation of Youth,* chapter 2)

Emotions: Signposts of Wellness

The physicians have commanded the observation of emotional changes and keeping them always under consideration—trying to equalize them in health or disease—without allowing any other behavior to take precedence. The physician must keep in mind that the heart of every sick person is narrow and that every healthy person has an expanded soul, and therefore the physician must remove emotional experiences that cause a shrinking of our spirit. In this way, the health of the normal person will be extended.

This is the law in the cure of a patient, especially if the illness is concentrated in the powers of the soul . . . and causes turbulent thoughts and melancholy.

Special care should be taken in observing emotional movements. When the patient is overpowered by imagination, prolonged introspection, and avoidance of social contact—all of which he never exhibited before—or when the patient avoids pleasant experiences that earlier were enjoyable, the physician should do nothing before first improving the soul by removing extreme emotions. (*The Preservation of Youth,* chapter 3)

A Perspective on Health

The physician as such will neither explore hyperemotionality with his wisdom nor condemn it. One can observe this point from philosophy and theoretical morality. Just as the philosophers have composed books in the various sciences, so they composed many books on the improvement of conduct, the soul's morality, and the imparting of good habits from which only good actions can result.

And they have warned against base habits that contribute to the causation of evil. All the theoretical moral teachings, chastisements, and precepts that are taken from the prophets, their preaching and character, or from later sages, as well as knowledge of virtuous behavior, will help to improve the soul's qualities until these reach such praiseworthy behavior that can produce only good results.

And you will find that those exaggerated emotions can produce changes only in the ignoble masses—who possess no

wisdom, no philosophical principles, and no theoretical morality, like children. All these timid souls are easily startled and
terrified. When injury befalls them or an inevitable misfortune
occurs to them, you will find that their consternation increases. They pine and cry and smite their faces and chests.
And it may happen that their feelings become so intense that
an ordinary person will die from them—immediately or later
—according to the grief and distress experienced. (*The Preservation of Youth,* chapter 3)

Recognize What's Trivial

As your servant, I have hinted all of this [that adversity is often
not as bad as it seems] to stir up and habituate your soul to
accept little things with a minimum of agitation. When you
follow the books on virtue and the morality of the teachings,
chastisements, and regulations composed by the sages, your
soul will become strengthened. You will recognize the meaningful: that it *is* meaningful. And you will recognize the trivial: that it *is* trivial. With the eye of the mind, your sad thoughts
will disappear. (*The Preservation of Youth,* chapter 3)

Foundations of Judaism

PRECISELY how Maimonides viewed Judaism, and his own mission regarding its place in the world, remains a fascinating question. It's also a highly complex one. Why? Because over the course of an influential life, his perspective not only kept evolving but also reflected wildly diverse intended audiences. These ranged from erudite rabbinic colleagues to ordinary Jews seeking to bolster their shaky faith and faltering communal identity to famous Muslim philosophers and rulers to suffering medical patients. We cannot possibly expect that a wise leader would offer the same religious message to them all. To do so is to fall into a trap that seems to have ensnared scholars for centuries through the present day.

It seems more productive, therefore, to find the Jewish "core" of Maimonides' soul not only in his extensive and sometimes contradictory writing but also in what psychology today calls biodata: his interests, activities, and accomplishments. What does such a fresh approach tell us? For reasons of brevity, three answers are most salient.

First, that Maimonides maintained an intense devotion to Judaism throughout his life. To the extent that his emotionally restrained temperament permitted, it was not only heartfelt but impassioned as well. From youth in Spain through steadily declining health in Egypt, his commitment to Jewish teachings was unflagging. It encompassed both scholarly and communal dimensions and never really shifted. His loyalty to Judaism as an embodied community of individuals with human flaws and frailties was equally unshakable.

Second, it's clear that Maimonides' particular attraction for Jewish tradition was primarily intellectual. Again, the issue of temperament is highly relevant, for scholarly activity—reading and engaging in commentary—was always his favorite pastime. Though as a physician he recommended music for its uplifting and curative power, there's no evidence that Maimonides ever composed liturgy, led his synagogues in songful worship, or played any musical instruments. Likewise, he never composed poems or even dabbled in poetry as a young man. In fact, historians believe it was the one subject he abhorred throughout his early education. In an Andalusian culture in which rabbis typically wrote with flowery imagery and metaphor even in matters of theology, Maimonides' penchant for precise prose well reveals his sober personality—and how it meshed with Judaism.

Finally, Maimonides was clearly drawn intellectually to non-Jewish sources throughout his life. No doubt this reflected his conviction that knowledge of the cosmos was hardly limited to Jews but accessible to all humanity. The notion sometimes advanced by historians that Maimonides became enamored with Greek philosophy only late in his career—when composing *Guide for the Perplexed*—is absurd. For by his early twenties, he had already written a careful introduction to logic in a treatise that contained nothing of Judaism. Association with prominent Muslim thinkers would only strengthen his view that truth can be universally grasped.

Such a view—especially in Maimonides' medieval milieu—would not have been incompatible in the least with the prophetic faith of Jewish commitment, redemption, and messianism that he unfailingly embraced.

TEACHINGS

The Divine Cosmos

Know that this universe, in its entirety, is nothing else but one individual Being. (*The Guide for the Perplexed,* book 1, chapter 72)

The God Force

There exists in the universe a certain force that controls the whole, that sets in motion the chief and principal parts and gives them the motive power for governing the rest. Without that force, the existence . . . of the universe would be impossible. It is the source of its existence in all of its parts. That force is God. (*The Guide for the Perplexed,* book 1, chapter 72)

———

God exists without having the attribute of existence. He is One without having the attribute of unity. (*The Guide for the Perplexed,* book 1, chapter 57)

Can God be Comprehended?

There is no possibility of obtaining knowledge of the true essence of God. . . . The only thing that humanity can comprehend of God is the fact that He exists. All positive attributes are inadmissible, as has been shown. (*The Guide for the Perplexed,* book 1, chapter 59)

———

A general principle to hold on to is that our finite mind cannot comprehend the nature of the Creator's judgment of the human individual in this world or in the World to Come. (*Letter to the Jews of Marseilles*)

———

God cannot be the object of human comprehension. None but God comprehends His essence. Our knowledge consists in knowing that we are unable to truly comprehend Him. (*The Guide for the Perplexed,* book 1, chapter 59)

Can God Be Described?

We cannot describe the Creator by any means except by negative attributes. Positive attributes ["God is good" or "God is merciful"] imply polytheism and are inadequate. (*The Guide for the Perplexed,* book 1, chapter 58)

———

Every time you establish by proof the negation of a thing in reference to God, you become more perfect, while with every additional positive assertion, you follow only your fantasies and recede from a true knowledge of God. (*The Guide for the Perplexed,* book 1, chapter 59)

———

It is a well-known fact that even that meager knowledge of God that is accessible to humanity cannot be attained except by negations. (*The Guide for the Perplexed,* book 1, chapter 59)

Angels

Belief in the existence of angels is connected with belief in the existence of God, and belief in God and angels leads to belief in prophecy and in the truth of Jewish law.

In order to firmly establish this creed, God commanded [the Israelites] to place over the ark the form of two angels. The belief in the existence of angels is thus inculcated into the minds of the people, and this belief is in importance next to the belief in God's existence: it leads us to believe in prophecy and in Jewish Law and opposes idolatry.

If there had been only one figure of a cherub, the people would have been misled and would have mistaken it for God's image—to be worshipped in the fashion of a heathen. Or they might have assumed that the angel [represented by the figure] was a deity, too, and would have adopted a Dualism.

By making two cherubim and distinctly declaring that "the Lord is our God, the Lord is One," Moses clearly proclaimed the existence of angels. He left no room for the error of considering these figures to be deities. (*The Guide for the Perplexed,* book 3, chapter 45)

The Value of Torah

Every narrative in the Torah serves a certain purpose in connection with religious teaching. It helps either to establish a principle of faith or to regulate our actions and to prevent wrong and injustice among people. (*The Guide for the Perplexed,* book 3, chapter 50)

———

Every Jew is required to study Torah, whether poor or rich, healthy or infirm, young or old and frail. Even a beggar who goes from door to door, and a man who has a wife and children to support, must devote time to Torah study during the day and at night. (*Mishneh Torah,* book 1, treatise 3, chapter 1:8)

———

The general object of the Torah is twofold: the well-being of the soul and the well-being of the body. The well-being of the soul is promoted by correct opinions communicated to people according to their capacity. Some of these opinions are imparted in a plain form, others allegorically. This is because certain opinions in their plain form are too strong for the capacity of ordinary folk.

The well-being of the body is established by a proper management of the relations in which we live one to another. This we can attain in two ways: first by removing all violence from our midst. That is to say, that we do not every one of us do as he pleases, desires, and is able to do, but every one of us does that which contributes toward the common good. Second, by teaching every one of us good morals as must produce a good social state. (*The Guide for the Perplexed,* book 3, chapter 27)

———

When should a parent begin to teach a child Torah? As soon as the child begins to talk, parents should teach the biblical verses "The Torah which Moses handed down to us" (Deuteronomy 33:4) and "Hear, O Israel" (Deuteronomy 6:4). Later on, parents should gradually teach their child more and more verses over time, until he reaches the age of six or seven. It all depends on the child's health. Parents should then take him to a teacher of young children. (*Mishneh Torah,* book 1, treatise 3, chapter 1:6)

Why We Need Rituals

We must bear in mind that all such religious acts as reading the Torah, praying, and performing other precepts serve exclusively as the means of causing us to occupy and fill our mind with the precepts of God—and free it from worldly business. For we are thus, as it were, in communication with God and undisturbed by any other thing. (*The Guide for the Perplexed,* book 2, chapter 51)

Jewish Devotion

Every Jew is required to sanctify God's name. (*Letter on Martyrdom*)

———

Any place inhabited by ten Jews should have a house of worship where they can assemble at all times of prayer. This is called a synagogue. The residents may compel one another to build a synagogue and buy a Torah scroll as well as the books of the prophets and the sacred writings. (*Mishneh Torah,* book 2, treatise 2, chapter 11:1)

———

Everything that is performed in the name of God must be of the best and finest. If one builds a house of prayer, it must be more beautiful than one's own house; if one feeds the hungry, one should give them the finest and best food of one's table; if one clothes the needy, one should give them the best one owns; if one dedicates something for a holy purpose, it should be of the best one possesses. (*Mishneh Torah,* book 1, treatise 5, chapter 3:2)

———

One should always pray for what is still to come and offer praise for past events, lauding and praising as much as possible. The more someone praises God at all times, the more praise he himself deserves. (*Mishneh Torah,* book 2, treatise 7, chapter 10:26)

Guidelines for Prayer

Concentration of the mind—how is this condition to be fulfilled? Any prayer uttered without mental concentration is not prayer. If a service has been recited without such concentration, it must be recited again devoutly. If a person finds that his thoughts are confused and his mind is distracted, he may not pray until he has recovered his mental composure. Hence, on returning from a journey or if one is very weary or distressed, it is forbidden to pray until his mind is composed. The sages said that he should wait three days until he is rested and his mind is calm, and then he recites the prayers. (*Mishneh Torah,* book 2, treatise 2, chapter 4:15)

———

What is to be understood as concentration of the mind? It should be freed from all extraneous thoughts, and the one who prays should realize that he is standing before the Divine Presence. . . . The ancient sages preferred to pause and meditate one hour before the service and one hour after the service, and take one hour in its recital. (*Mishneh Torah,* book 2, treatise 2, chapter 4:16)

———

An intoxicated person must not pray, because he cannot concentrate. . . . So, too, persons should not stand up to pray after indulging in jest, laughter, frivolity, idle talk, quarreling, or outbursts of anger. (*Mishneh Torah,* book 2, treatise 2, chapter 4:17–18)

The Sacred Sabbath

The Sabbath is an eternal sign between the Holy One, blessed be He, and ourselves. (*Mishneh Torah,* book 3, treatise 1, chapter 30:15)

———

The basic intent of observing the Sabbath is that we sanctify ourselves through involvement in spiritual activities, marking the day when God completed creation as the day for the perfection of our souls by ceasing from worldly affairs, travel, and work. In this way we come to know God—and this constitutes the most perfect and true form of repose. Hence, rest on the Sabbath is of a twofold nature: physical and mental. (Letter on Ethics to Son, Abraham)

———

The objective of Sabbath is obvious and requires no explanation. The rest it affords to the individual is known: one-seventh of the life of every person—whether lowly or great—passes thus in comfort and in rest from trouble and exertion. (*The Guide for the Perplexed,* book 3, chapter 43)

———

Lovemaking is regarded as Sabbath's delight. Accordingly, scholars in good health should fulfill their conjugal obligation every Friday night. (*Mishneh Torah,* book 3, treatise 1, chapter 30:14)

———

What is Sabbath's delight? This is explained by the statement of the sages that one should prepare for the Sabbath the choicest foods and beverages that one can afford. The more one spends for the Sabbath, and for the preparation of numerous and tasty dishes, the more praiseworthy he is.

If, however, one cannot afford this, it is sufficient to make the Sabbath a delight by preparing even a plain vegetable stew or the like. For one is not obligated to humiliate himself by begging from others in order to provide a large quantity of food for the Sabbath. (*Mishneh Torah,* book 3, treatise 1, chapter 30:7)

———

Prolonged idle conversation is forbidden on the Sabbath, for when Scripture says, "Nor speaking thereof" (Isaiah 58:13), it indicates that one's Sabbath conversation should not be the same as on weekdays. (*Mishneh Torah,* book 3, treatise 1, chapter 23:4)

———

On the Sabbath, a father may carry a child who longs to be so carried, even if the child has a pebble in his hands. But not if he has a dinar in his hand, for should he drop the coin, the father is likely to pick it up. (*Mishneh Torah,* book 3, treatise 1, chapter 23:16)

———

One is forbidden on the Sabbath to go anywhere in connection with his business or even to talk about it. Thus one may not discuss with his partner what to sell on the next day or what to buy or how to construct a certain house or what merchandise to take to a particular place. All such speech is forbidden. (*Mishneh Torah,* book 3, treatise 1, chapter 24:1)

Fasting for the Jewish Community

A positive scriptural commandment prescribes prayer and the sounding of an alarm with trumpets whenever trouble befalls a Jewish community. For when Scripture says, "Against the adversary that oppresses you, then you shall sound an alarm with the trumpets" (Numbers 10:9), the meaning is: Cry out in prayer and sound an alarm against whatever is oppressing you, whether famine, pestilence, locusts, or the like. (*Mishneh Torah,* book 3, treatise 9, chapter 1:1)

————

On the authority of the scribes, fasting is required whenever trouble befalls a Jewish community, until mercy from heaven is provided for it. (*Mishneh Torah,* book 3, treatise 9, chapter 1:4)

————

The following are the afflictions for which a Jewish community should fast and sound an alarm: oppression by their enemies, war, pestilence, wild beasts, locusts, crickets, blasting of crops, mildew, collapse of buildings, epidemics, economic crisis, and excess or deficiency of rain.

Whenever a city suffers one of the aforementioned calamities, it should fast and sound the alarm until the trouble is past. All neighboring cities should also fast, but without sounding an alarm, and should pray for mercy on behalf of the afflicted city. (*Mishneh Torah,* book 3, treatise 9, chapter 2:1–2)

The Sanctity of Human Life

The commandment of the Sabbath, like all other commandments, must be set aside if human life is in danger. Accordingly, if a person is dangerously ill, whatever a skilled local physician considers necessary must be done for him on the Sabbath.

If it is uncertain whether the Sabbath needs to be violated or not—if one physician says that violation is necessary and another says that it's not—the Sabbath should be violated, for the mere possibility of danger to human life overrides the Sabbath. (*Mishneh Torah,* book 3, treatise 1, chapter 2:1)

———

If a building collapses and there is a possibility that a human being was inside it, the debris may be cleared away to search for him. If he is found alive, whether even so severely injured that recovery is impossible, one must nevertheless continue the effort to extricate him and save his life, however short it may prove to be. (*Mishneh Torah,* book 3, treatise 1, chapter 2:18)

———

If a ship is storm-tossed at sea, or if a city is surrounded by marauding troops or by a flooding river, it is a religious duty to go to the people's rescue on the Sabbath and to use every means to deliver them. (*Mishneh Torah,* book 3, treatise 1, chapter 1:24)

———

If a person who is dangerously ill asks for food on Yom Kippur, it should be given to him in accordance with his request, until he himself says he has had enough—even if expert physicians say he does not need any. If the patient says that he does not require any food, while the physician says that he does, he should be given the food ordered by the physician, provided that the latter is an expert. If one physician says that the patient needs food, while another physician says that he does not, he should be fed. (*Mishneh Torah,* book 3, treatise 3, chapter 2:8)

———

If a court gave a wrong decision in a capital case, declaring an innocent person guilty and passing sentence on him for conviction, and later discovered a reason for reversing the sentence so as to clear the accused, the decision of the court is revoked and he is tried again.

If, however, the judges gave a wrong decision and acquitted one who deserved death, the decision is not revoked, and he is not brought back for a new trial. (*Mishneh Torah,* book 14, treatise 1, chapter 10:9)

———

A Noahide [ethical monotheist], even if he kills an embryo in the mother's womb, is put to death. So, too, if he kills someone suffering from a fatal disease or ties a man with a rope and puts him before a lion or leaves him in a famished condition in consequence of which the man dies of starvation, he is executed.

For in the last analysis, he caused the death of the victim. (*Mishneh Torah,* book 14, treatise 5, chapter 9:4)

On Suicide

For one who committed suicide, no funeral rites are performed, no mourning is observed, no lamentation is made. But the relatives stand in line [to be comforted], the Mourner's Benediction is recited, and all that is intended as a matter of honor for the living is due.

Who is to be regarded as a suicide? Not he who climbing up to the roof fell and died, but one who said: "Look, I am climbing to the top of the roof!"

If he was seen ascending it, agitated by anger or fear, and then fell and died, the presumption is that he committed suicide. (*Mishneh Torah,* book 14, treatise 4, chapter 1:11)

Respecting Non-Jews

As to your questions about non-Jews, know that the Lord desires the heart [kindness], and that the intention of the heart is the measure of all things. That is why our sages say, "The pious among the Gentiles have a share in the World to Come" (Sanhedrin 105a) namely, if they have acquired [adequate] knowledge of God and if they ennoble their souls with worthy qualities. (Letter to Hasdai Ha-Levi)

The Eight Rungs of Charity

There are right degrees of charity, one higher than another. The highest degree, exceeded by none, is that of the person who assists a poor Jew by providing him with a gift or a loan or by accepting him into a business partnership or by helping him find employment—in short, by placing him where he can dispense with other people's aid. With reference to such aid, it is said: "You shall strengthen him; be he a stranger or a settler, he shall live with you" (Leviticus 25:35), which means strengthen him in such a manner that his falling into want is prevented.

A step below this stands the one who gives alms to the needy in such manner that the giver knows not to whom he gives and the recipient knows not from whom it is that he receives. Such exemplifies performing the meritorious act for its own sake. An illustration would be the Hall of Secrecy in the ancient sanctuary, where the righteous would place their gift clandestinely and where poor people of illustrious ancestry would come and secretly help themselves.

The rank next to this is that of he who drops money in the charity box. One should not do so unless certain that the person in charge is trustworthy, wise, and competent to handle the funds properly. . . .

One step lower is that in which the giver knows to whom he gives, but the poor person knows not from whom he receives. Examples of this were the great sages who would go forth and covertly throw coins into poor people's doorways. This method becomes fitting and exalted, should it happen that those in charge of the charity fund do not conduct its affairs properly.

A step lower is that in which the poor person knows from whom he is receiving, but the giver knows not to whom he is giving. Examples of this were the great sages who would tie their coins in their scarves, which they would fling over their shoulders so that the poor might help themselves without suffering shame.

The next degree lower is that of one who, with his own hand, bestows a gift *before* the poor person asks.

The next degree lower is that of one who gives only *after* the poor person asks.

The next degree lower is that of one who gives less than is appropriate but gives with a gracious demeanor.

The next degree lower is that of one who gives morosely. (*Mishneh Torah,* book 7, treatise 1, chapter 10:7–15)

Be Generous in Charity

We have never seen or heard of a Jewish community without a charity fund. (*Mishneh Torah,* book 7, treatise 1, chapter 9:3)

———

It is preferable to spend more on gifts to the poor than on the Purim meal or on Purim presents to friends. For no joy is greater or more glorious than the joy of gladdening the hearts of the poor, the orphans, the widows, and the strangers. Indeed, he who causes the hearts of these unfortunates to rejoice emulates the Divine Presence. (*Mishneh Torah,* book 3, treatise 10, chapter 2:17)

———

We should observe the laws of charity more carefully even than all the other commandments. Charity (*zedakah*) is the mark of the righteous of the posterity of Abraham our Father, of whom it is said: "For I have known him to the end that he may command his children and his household after him, that they may keep the way of the Lord, to practice righteousness and justice" (Genesis 18:19). The throne of Israel and the religion of truth is based only on *zedakah*. And only because of *zedakah* will Israel be redeemed, as it is said: "Zion shall be redeemed by justice, and those in her who repent, by righteousness (*zedakah*)" (Isaiah 1:27). (*Mishneh Torah*, book 7, treatise 1, chapter 10:1)

———

None ever becomes poor from giving charity. No harm or evil can be the outcome of it. He who has compassion for others is deserving of compassion. As to the merciless one who knows no pity, his Jewish extraction may be considered doubtful, because cruelty is usually a characteristic of pagans. Jews and those who join them are brothers to one another, and it is said of them: "Ye are the children of the Lord your God" (Deuteronomy 14:1). If a brother does not commiserate with his brother, who, then, should pity him? (*Mishneh Torah*, book 7, treatise 1, chapter 10:2)

———

If a poor man requests money from you and you have nothing to give him, speak to him consolingly. (*Mishneh Torah*, book 7, treatise 1, chapter 10:5)

———

It is forbidden to scold a poor person or to shout at him, because his heart is broken. (*Mishneh Torah*, book 7, treatise 1, chapter 10:5)

———

Whoever gives charity to a poor person ill-manneredly and arrogantly has lost all the merit of his action even though he gives a thousand gold pieces. He should give with good grace and joy and sympathize with him in his plight. He should offer words of consolation and sympathy. (*Mishneh Torah,* book 7, treatise 1, chapter 10:4)

Honoring Your Parents

The honoring of father and mother is a weighty positive commandment; so, too, is reverence for them. The Bible attaches to the duty of honoring and revering parents an importance equal to that which it attaches to the duty of honoring and revering God.

In the matter of honor due to parents, the father is mentioned first. In the matter of reverence due to them, the mother is mentioned first. From this we infer that both are to be equally honored and revered.

What does reverence imply? What does honor imply? Reverence requires that the son should not stand in the place his father usually stands or sit in his place or contradict his words or decide against his opinion or call him, living or dead, by his name. . . .

What does honoring parents imply? It means providing them with food and drink, clothing and covering, the expense to be borne by the son. If the father is poor and the son is in a position to take care of his parents, he is compelled to do so. He must support his parents in accordance with his means, conduct his father in and out, and perform for him such personal services as disciples perform for their teacher. He rises before him, as he rises before his teacher. (*Mishneh Torah,* book 14, treatise 3, chapter 6:3)

When a Parent Has Dementia

If the mind of one's father or mother is afflicted, the son should make every effort to indulge the vagaries of the stricken parent until God will have mercy on the afflicted. But if the condition of the parent has grown worse—and the son is no longer able to endure the strain—he may leave the father or the mother, go elsewhere, and delegate others to give the parent proper care. (*Mishneh Torah,* book 14, treatise 3, chapter 6:10)

Relating to Other Jews

It is not right to alienate, scorn, and hate people who desecrate the Sabbath. It is our duty to befriend them and encourage them to fulfill the commandments. (*Letter on Martyrdom*)

———

The rabbis say explicitly that when a sinner by choice comes to the synagogue, he is to be welcomed. (*Letter on Martyrdom*)

Maimonides' View of His Judaic Works

I try to reconcile Jewish law and reason and, whenever possible, consider that all things are of the natural order. Only when something is explicitly identified as a miracle and reinterpretation of it cannot be accommodated, only then do I feel forced to grant that this is a miracle. *(Letter on Resurrection)*

———

All of you who have read my works know well that I always aim to avoid disagreements and challenges. If I could squeeze the entire law of the Torah into one chapter, I would not write two chapters for it. (*Letter on Resurrection*)

———

I did not write my *Mishneh Torah* in order to excel or to be glorified by my fellow Jews. The Almighty knows that my original effort in writing the book was directed toward my own personal use. I wanted to be relieved of the involved investigations and subtle intricacies required to discover a necessary point. When I grew older, I became aware that my people were without a comprehensive book of law that would embrace definitive concepts without controversies and textual errors. (Letter to Joseph ibn Aknin)

The Thirteen Articles of Faith

Our religion is based on the following thirteen principles:

The first fundamental principle. The first principle is to believe in the existence of the Creator, that there is an Existent complete in all aspects of the word "existence." He is the cause of all existence. . . . This principle is taught in the biblical verse "I am the Lord your God" (Exodus 20:2).

The second fundamental principle. We are told to believe that God is one, the cause of all oneness. He is not like a member of a pair nor a species of a genus nor a person divided into many discrete parts. Nor is He one in the sense that a single body is, necessarily, numerically one but still infinitely divisible. God, rather, is uniquely one. This principle is taught in the biblical verse "Hear, O Israel, the Lord our God, the Lord is One" (Deuteronomy 6:4).

The third fundamental principle. We are to believe that God is incorporeal, that His unity is physical neither potentially nor actually. None of the attributes of matter can be predicated of Him. . . . This principle is taught in the biblical verse "You have seen no image" (Deuteronomy 4:15).

The fourth fundamental principle. We are to believe that the One is absolutely eternal, no thing existed before Him. . . . This principle is taught in the biblical verse "A dwelling place is the Eternal God" (Deuteronomy 33:27).

The fifth fundamental principle. Only He, blessed be He, is rightfully worshipped, exalted, and obeyed. One must not pray to anything beneath Him in existence: angels, stars, planets, or elements or anything composed of these. . . . This principle has all biblical warnings against idolatry as its warrant: in other words, the bulk of the Torah.

The sixth fundamental principle. Prophecy is the sixth principle: One should know that among humanity are found those so gifted and perfected that they receive pure intellectual form. Their human intellect clings to the Active Intellect and is thereby gloriously raised. . . . I remind you in passing of the many scriptural passages that testify to the prophecy of many different prophets.

The seventh fundamental principle. The prophecy of Moses, our Teacher, is the seventh principle. We are to believe that he was the chief of all other prophets before and after him, all of whom were his inferiors. . . . He surpassed the normal human condition and attained the angelic. . . . Moses's prophecy was [superior to] that of all other prophets in four respects. . . .

The eighth fundamental principle. The Torah came from God. We are to believe that the whole Torah was given us through Moses our Teacher entirely from God. When we call the Torah "God's Word" we speak metaphorically. We do not know exactly how it reached us, but only that it came to us through Moses, who acted like a secretary taking dictation. . . .

Every word of Torah is full of wisdom and wonders for one who understands it. It is beyond human comprehension. It is broader than the earth and wider than the sea. . . . This fundamental principle is taught by the verse "And Moses said: 'Thus shall you know that the Lord sent me to do all of these things, and that they are not products of my own mind'" (Numbers 16:28).

The ninth fundamental principle. The ninth principle is the authenticity of the Torah: that is, that this Torah was precisely transcribed from God and no one else. To the Torah, oral and written, nothing must be added or deleted. . . .

The tenth fundamental principle. God knows all that individuals do and never turns His eyes away from them—contrary to those who claim "the Lord has abandoned this earth" (Ezekiel 8:12, 9:9). Rather, as Scripture has it, "Great in counsel, mighty in insight [is] God, whose eyes are open to all the ways of humanity" (Jeremiah 32:19). . . .

The eleventh fundamental principle. God rewards those who perform the commandments of the Torah and punishes those who transgress its admonitions. The greatest reward is the World to Come; the worst punishment is extinction. We have already made this sufficiently clear. . . .

The twelfth fundamental principle. The twelfth principle refers to the Messianic Age. We are to believe as fact that the Messiah will come and not consider him late. If he delays, wait for him (Habakkuk 2:3). Set no time limit for his coming. One must not make conjectures based on Scripture when the Messiah will come. . . .

The thirteenth fundamental principle. The thirteenth principle is the resurrection of the dead, which we have already explained. (Introduction to Perek Herek, *Sanhedrin*)

Kindness to Animals

One who borrows an animal is obliged to feed it from the moment he draws it to himself until the end of the term for which he borrowed it. (*Mishneh Torah,* book 8, treatise 2, chapter 1:4)

Intriguing Children about Passover

On the first night of Passover, one should introduce some change at the table, so that the children, who will notice it, may ask, "Why is this night different from all other nights?" And he in turn will reply: "This is what happened."

In what manner, for example, should he introduce a change? By distributing parched grain or nuts to the children or by removing the table from its usual place or by each trying to snatch the other's matzo, and so on. If he has no son, his wife should ask the question. If he has no wife, those at the table should ask one another, "Why is this night different?" even if they are all scholars. If one is alone, he should ask himself, "Why is this night different?" (*Mishneh Torah,* book 3, treatise 5, chapter 7:3)

Canceling an Oath

What is the procedure for an absolution? The swearer must appear before an outstanding scholar, or before three ordinary men where no expert is available, and say: "I swore an oath concerning such-and-such a matter, and now I regret it. Had I known that I would be in such distress through it, or that such-and-such a thing would happen to me, I would not have sworn," or "Had I been of the same mind at the time of swearing as I am now, I would not have sworn."

The sage, or the senior of the three consultants, should then say to him: "And do you indeed regret it?" And he should reply, "Yes." Whereupon the sage should say to him, "You are released" or "absolved" or "pardoned" or something to the same effect in any language.

But if he says, "It is now revoked for you" or "Your oath is eradicated" or anything with a similar meaning, his words are of no effect. For only a husband or a father can revoke an oath; a sage may speak only in terms of absolution or pardon. (*Mishneh Torah,* book 6, treatise 1, chapter 6:5)

Avoid Hasty Oaths

Anyone who says to his companions, "Let us rise early and study a chapter of Mishnah" is bound to do so, for this counts

as a vow—even though it was not expressed in terms of a vow.
(*Mishneh Torah*, book 6, treatise 2, chapter 1:29)

The Oaths of Children

Boys who are twelve years and one day old and girls who are
eleven years and one day old who have sworn an oath or
made a vow—whether a vow of prohibition or consecration—should be examined and interrogated. If they understand in whose name they vowed, consecrated, or swore, their
vows are binding and their consecration is effective. If not,
their vows are words of no effect. They must be examined
concerning each individual vow throughout the whole of the
year: that is, the twelfth year in the case of a girl and the thirteenth year in the case of a boy. (*Mishneh Torah*, book 6, treatise 2, chapter 11:1)

Don't Make Deceptive Claims

It is forbidden to deceive people in buying and selling or to
deceive them by creating a false impression.

A heathen and an Israelite are to be treated alike in this
respect.

If one knows that an article he is selling has a defect, he
must inform the buyer about it.

It is forbidden to deceive people even by words. (*Mishneh
Torah*, book 12, treatise 1, chapter 18:1–3)

Protecting the Environment

Carcasses, graves, and tanneries must be kept fifty cubits from
the town. (*Mishneh Torah*, book 12, treatise 3, chapter 10:3)

Gamblers

A dice player is disqualified from giving evidence in court if he has no other occupation. In view of the fact that he contributes nothing to the welfare of society, the presumption is that he makes his living out of dice playing, which is a form of robbery. The rule holds good not only for those who play with dice but also for those who play with nutshells and pomegranate peels. (*Mishneh Torah,* book 14, treatise 2, chapter 10:4)

Be Careful in Accepting Self-Incrimination

No man becomes ineligible to give evidence in court on his own admission of religious delinquency. For example, if a person appears in court and says that he has stolen or robbed, or loaned money on interest, although he has to make restitutions on his own admission, he is not disqualified as a witness. Two witnesses must testify against him, for no man can incriminate himself. (*Mishneh Torah,* book 14, treatise 2, chapter 22:2)

The Importance of Visiting the Sick

Everyone is duty-bound to visit the sick. Even a man of prominence must visit a less important person. The ill should be visited many times a day. The more often a person calls on the sick, the more praiseworthy is he, provided that he does not inconvenience the patient. One who visits the sick is as though removing part of the illness and lightening the pain.

Whoever does not call to see the sick is as though he would shed blood. (*Mishneh Torah,* book 14, treatise 4, chapter 14:4)

The Nature of Repentance (Teshuvah)

When we commit a sin, we must atone for it, as must our children and grandchildren, by some kind of service analogous to the sin committed. If a person has sinned with respect to property, he must liberally spend his property in God's service. If he indulged in sinful bodily enjoyments, he must weary his body by a service of privation, fasting, and rising early, before daybreak. If he went astray with respect to his moral conduct, he must oppose his failings by keeping to the opposite extreme, as I have pointed out in *Mishneh Torah*.

If his intellectual faculties have been concerned with sin—if he has believed something false on account of intellectual inadequacy by failing properly to research and study—he must remedy his fault by turning his thoughts entirely away from worldly affairs and directing them exclusively to intellectual activity and by carefully reflecting on what should form the subject of his belief. (*The Guide for the Perplexed,* book 3, chapter 46)

Determining Whether Repentance Is Genuine

When may usurers be considered to have repented? When they tear up their notes of their own accord and undergo a thorough reformation so that they will not advance money on interest even to a heathen.

When may dice players be deemed to have repented? When they break up their blocks of wood and undergo a complete reformation—desisting even from playing as a pastime. (*Mishneh Torah,* book 14, treatise 2, chapter 12:6)

The Messianic Age

Let no one think that in the days of the Messiah, any of the laws of nature will be set aside or any innovation be introduced into creation. The world will follow its normal course. The words of Isaiah "And the wolf shall dwell with the lamb, and the leopard shall lie down with the kid" [Isaiah 11:6] are to be understood figuratively, meaning that Israel will live securely. (*Mishneh Torah,* book 14, treatise 5, chapter 12:1)

———

Some of our sages say that the coming of Elijah will precede the advent of the Messiah. But no one is in a position to know the details of this and similar things until they have come to pass. They are not explicitly stated by the prophets. Nor have the rabbis any tradition with regard to these matters. They are guided by what the scriptural texts seem to imply. Hence there is great diversity of opinion on the subject.

Be that as it may, neither the exact sequence of those events nor the details thereof constitute religious dogma. No one should ever occupy himself with the legendary themes or spend much time on midrashic statements bearing on this and like subjects. He should not deem them of prime importance. . . . Nor should one calculate the end. (*Mishneh Torah,* book 14, treatise 5, chapter 12:1)

———

In messianic times, all the Prophetic Books and the Writings (*Ketubim*) will cease to be used, except the book of Esther. For this will continue to endure, just as the Five Books of Moses and the rules of the Oral Law will never be rescinded. And so, all memories of ancient troubles will disappear. (*Mishneh Torah,* book 3, treatise 10 chapter 2:18)

———

In that era, there will be neither famine nor war, neither jealousy nor strife. Blessings will be abundant, comforts within the reach of all. The one preoccupation of the whole world will be to know the Lord. Hence Israelites will be very wise; they will know the things that are now concealed and will attain an understanding of their Creator to the utmost capacity of the human mind. As it is written, "For the earth shall be full of the knowledge of the Lord, as the waters cover the sea" (Isaiah 11:9). (*Mishneh Torah,* book 14, treatise 5, chapter 12:5)

PART THREE

VISIONARY TALES

INTRODUCTION TO THE
VISIONARY TALES OF
MAIMONIDES

AMAZINGLY, Maimonides ranks alongside such figures as the prophet Elijah as the subject of countless legends and folktales. It's easy to see why this holy biblical figure—mythologically transformed into an interceding angel who visits every Passover household—has enchanted Judaism's psyche for millennia. But how do we explain Rabbi Moses ben Maimon's immense and enduring popularity?

After all, he was a highly disciplined scholar who condemned mass excitements like astrology and led no grassroots movements. After moving to Egypt, he spent most of his ensuing life in upper-class circles, both Jewish and Muslim. Even his Córdoba background was elite. While imbued with marvelous clarity, his writing offered few imaginative or even poetic flights to transport everyday Jews into dreamy consciousness.

Yet it seems altogether reasonable that Maimonides—unlike other venerated scholars—indeed became a mythological figure to world Jewry. Two explanations appear both sensible and historically relevant. First, Rabbi Moses ben Maimon was a true leader who offered hope and encouragement to beleaguered Jewish communities around the globe. He was not simply a pedant. From an early age, he showed initiative, boldness, and integrity. He was also a visionary who saw a bright future ahead when most fellow Jews perceived only darkness. Certainly such admirable qualities are the essential "stuff" of legend.

Second, Maimonides was indisputably the leading Jewish "celebrity" of his era—one who succeeded in overcoming great hardship to achieve a position of unequaled fame and influence. As physician to Saladin's court, he was not only renowned as a brilliant healer but also cordial with the most powerful men of the Islamic world. Like biblical Joseph, who rose from slavery and prison to become the pharaoh's viceroy, Maimonides reached a remarkable summit. Nevertheless, he remained totally loyal to his own heritage. Is it really any wonder that his life took on fabulous color over time?

The eleven diverse tales presented here are representative of those that have flourished—often in oral form—among the Jews of Afghanistan, Bulgaria, England, Egypt, Hungary, Iraq, Lithuania, Morocco, Poland, Romania, Tunisia, Turkey, Yemen, and many other countries. It's impossible to say, of course, how much truth lies behind each story. What's interesting and noteworthy is that they highlight aspects of Maimonides' personality—especially humor and wit alongside human insight—typically missing from religious and philosophical portraits through the centuries.

I

THE LOST CHILD

ONE DAY when Moses was still a little boy, he lost his way in Córdoba. A ship carried him off, along with the crew, to another country. Moses had brought with him a little booklet that was never far from his lips.

After disembarking in a strange city, young Moses began to roam through the streets. He followed no particular course. Thus he was discovered by guards who were making their rounds, and they took him to the city's prince. The monarch didn't know how to communicate with the boy, as he didn't know his language. But suddenly Moses showed him the booklet he was holding: it was none other than a portion of the Torah.

The prince understood that a Jewish child stood before him and immediately ordered that he be returned to Córdoba. All along, Moses firmly clutched his beloved booklet.

When Moses was finally reunited with his father, Rabbi Maimon fell before the booklet and kissed it, wetting it with the joyful tears he was shedding. At that precise moment, little Moses made a vow to write his work *Mishneh Torah*.

2

A WELL-BALANCED DIET

THE RAMBAM once had a loyal servant, Eliezer, who carried out his orders conscientiously. One day Maimonides said to him: "From now on, please bring me two onions every morning."

And every morning, the Rambam would eat the onions on an empty stomach. When Eliezer saw this, he said to himself: "If my master, who is a famous doctor, takes two onions every morning, then surely they must contain a healing remedy."

So what did Eliezer do? He too began eating onions every morning, but instead of two, he decided to take four—to gain twice the benefit.

Time passed. One day the Rambam climbed to the roof of his house and found his servant there, gazing far into the distance. He asked: "What do you see there?"

"I am watching a man riding on his horse," was the reply.

As the Rambam could discern neither horse nor rider, he

grasped that Eliezer was also eating onions every morning on an empty stomach, but not the proper amount.

After they descended, Maimonides called Eliezer into his room and said: "Instead of the onions that you serve me every morning, please bring me hot peppers."

The next day Eliezer brought him hot peppers, while saying to himself, "If the Rambam, who is a famous physician, is no longer eating onions but now hot peppers, then surely they must have healing powers." Meanwhile, Maimonides would put aside the peppers and continue to take his ration of two onions each morning.

Thus the days went by, with the servant eating hot peppers while the Rambam ate his onions. Then one day Maimonides asked Eliezer to accompany him to the roof of the house and asked:

"Can you see the bull over there, that's walking right across the street?"

"No, I don't see any bull over there," the servant replied. The entire street appeared hazy to him.

"Tell me the truth," firmly asked the Rambam, "how many onions were you eating daily?"

"Four a day," Eliezer replied.

"And why didn't you consult me first?"

"Why should I have done so?" asked the surprised servant.

"Because the onion is a very strong remedy. It contains a substance that is good for eyesight, but only if it is taken in the right amount. So if you had kept on eating four onions every morning, you would eventually have gone blind. As for the hot peppers, you should have asked me about them, too. I put aside the hot peppers you gave me and continued to eat the onions. But you took too much of the one as well as the other, for the peppers have been affecting your eyesight."

"And now what should I do?" asked a worried Eliezer.

"Take neither onions nor peppers until I see that your eyesight has returned to normal. And next time, ask me before you follow the dietary regimen I choose."

Eliezer instantly agreed, and before long his eyesight returned to normal. And whenever he saw the Rambam following a certain dietary regimen, Eliezer asked if it was advisable for him, too.

3

THE UNNECESSARY
EXORCISM

W HILE THE Rambam was living in Egypt, he directed an unusual incident of healing. It involved
an elderly Christian woman, Sophia, who was suffering from dangerously high fevers that caused her to lapse
into a state of deep lethargy.

All of her lifetime, Sophia had never learned to read or
write in any language. But when the illness assailed her, she
would suddenly begin to speak loudly in Latin, Greek, and
even Hebrew. Therefore the suspicion grew among the people in her household that Sophia was possessed by a demon.
As there arose a great commotion in town, the Rambam was
called in to perform an exorcism and to prescribe remedies to
cast out the demon.

When Maimonides arrived and heard what was happening,
he ordered that everything the patient said be written down

exactly, on sheets of paper. The result was a thick sheaf of papers. Once it was bundled and organized, it was clear that Sophia was uttering phrases in Latin and Greek of profound wisdom and understanding—though no relation existed between one phrase and the next.

As far as Sophia's Hebrew utterances were concerned, they were all either verses from the Holy Torah, or from well-known commentaries on morals. Yet this elderly woman was definitely illiterate, lacking even the most basic schooling.

The Rambam resolved to clear up this matter and discover the secret that lay behind it. He began to make inquiries and question Sophia's family as to where she had spent her childhood. After intensive investigation, Maimonides learned that when Sophia was nine years old, she had resided in the home of a priest whose study chamber was adjacent to the kitchen quarters where she lived and worked.

Reportedly, the priest was accustomed to pace the floor while reciting passages from the Torah and from books on morals in the diverse languages in which he was proficient.

The Rambam then went to look through the priest's library, which was still intact. The exact words that Sophia was uttering in her high fevers were easily found among his books and commentaries.

After this matter was cleared up, the Rambam explained to Sophia's amazed family that she was not possessed by any demon. Rather, the high fever had brought back the old words that had reached Sophia's ears as a child long ago. Although she did not understand their meaning, she had retained them in memory all of these years.

Then the Rambam prescribed a remedy for Sophia, and soon she was completely cured.

4

A Cure for Depression

After Maimonides had been court physician to Saladin for several years, the sultan's eldest son, al-Afdal, fell into a deep depression. He was a young man long known for his self-indulgent and dissolute ways. The sultan brought his greatest and most talented jesters and courtesans, and finally astrologers and soothsayers, to heal al-Afdal, but all to no avail. His depression worsened.

When word reached Maimonides about this calamity, he quickly offered to intervene, but Saladin's ministers sharply rebuffed him. They wanted no heathen Jew to treat Saladin's eldest son—their future ruler. Saladin followed their advice.

Meanwhile, al-Afdal grew weaker with every passing week. He stopped bathing altogether, as well as taking strolls in the royal gardens so famous throughout the world for their elegance and beauty. Each day he hardly roused from his bedchamber—and did so only to taste a tiny morsel from the sumptuous banquet brought to his inner chambers before wordlessly shaking his head and then shakily returning to bed.

Nobody could lift al-Afdal from his sinking depression, and nobody could even explain what had befallen the sultan's beloved son. Wizards and miracle workers from far away were dutifully summoned, but none could effect the slightest cure.

Saladin was loath to let Maimonides grapple with his eldest son's illness. But finally there was no choice. Saladin's closest advisers all agreed that the Jewish physician was now the only hope left, for al-Afdal's mental and physical condition were swiftly deteriorating to the point of no return.

Upon being summoned by the sultan's personal messenger, Maimonides immediately came to the royal palace. He requested that al-Afdal be brought to the medical examination room. About an hour passed, and then, surrounded by his prized guards, Saladin's son appeared. Barely standing erect, he stared vacantly at the renowned Jewish physician and said nothing in response to his cordial greetings.

Maimonides physically examined al-Afdal for what seemed liked hours to everyone in the room and then suddenly slapped the young prince hard across the face, twice. "Do you *still* feel depressed?" he asked.

Instantly al-Afdal's hollow expression changed to fury. His cheeks were red from the forceful blows. As the royal guards rushed to seize Maimonides for the impudence—whose punishment was to be burned alive—Saladin's son loudly replied, surprised, "No, my depression is gone." The sultan's ministers ordered the guards out of the room, and Saladin himself soon entered to embrace his eldest son, whose face was still a simmering bright red. But for the first time in many months, there was a smile across his lips and his eyes twinkled with life.

Later, to the astonished ministers, Maimonides explained: "The sultan's son leads a life of utmost luxury, but he must not live only in sensual pleasure and indulgence, for grief and joy were handed down from the Almighty closely intertwined— and we need them both. That is why I slapped the king's face, so that he would grow angry and his fury dispel the depression from his heart."

And in the days that followed, Maimonides' fame as a healer increased even more widely in lands both near and far.

5

HEALING THROUGH TEARS

IT CAME TO pass that Rabbi Abraham ben David of
Provence—a famous bitter foe of Maimonides—was
stricken with a serious eye disease. His friends advised
him to travel to Fustat, near Cairo in Egypt, to consult with
his rabbinic opponent. But Rabbi Abraham refused to see the
man whom he regarded as a renegade and an apostate. Finally,
as Rabbi Abraham's condition was badly worsening and de-
scending to near blindness, he agreed to his friends' entreaties
and made the distant journey to Cairo. While traveling, he
disguised his identity and posed as a simple worker.

As is well known, when Maimonides came home after a
long day's work at the royal court, he would wash his hands, eat
a light meal, and then walk along between two lines of patients
who were already waiting for him in orderly queues.

As was his custom, Maimonides looked carefully into the
eyes of each patient in order to determine the illness. When he
reached Rabbi Abraham and gazed into his luminous eyes,

Maimonides immediately realized that an illustrious person was present. And so, after examining all of his patients, Maimonides invited him to his workroom to have a closer look at his eyes. While making the examination, he began conversing with his patient, and, jumping from one topic to the next, they started delving into matters of Torah scholarship and philosophy. Before long Maimonides realized that the seemingly ordinary worker was none other than Rabbi Abraham ben David, but he said nothing in recognition.

After completing the initial checkup, Maimonides invited Rabbi Abraham to be his guest at home for several days in order to achieve a more thorough assessment. Rabbi Abraham felt obliged to agree in hopes of a cure but seethed inwardly. He certainly had no desire to become personally acquainted with this physician whose Torah writings seemed so abhorrent for their lack of conventional piety.

All during that week, Maimonides and his household deliberately acted in a manner to provoke Rabbi Abraham's anger. They repeatedly brought him foods and beverages that were not to his liking, made loud noises that disturbed his concentration, and pretended not to hear his various requests.

When the Sabbath arrived, Maimonides behaved in a strange and exasperating manner, arousing increasing irritability in Rabbi Abraham. But feeling obligated to observe the Sabbath's peace and sanctity, he restrained himself mightily and did not say a single negative word. Only after the Sabbath ended, when he could no longer hold himself back, did Rabbi Abraham explode with anger as Maimonides and his household listened impassively.

Yelling with rage, Rabbi Abraham poured out his soul's bitterness for everything that he had seen and heard during the entire week, and especially during the Sabbath, including Maimonides' eccentric actions. Suddenly, in the midst of this agitation, Rabbi Abraham's tear ducts burst open and from his eyes streamed tears and blood. Immediately he felt great relief in his eyes.

After his patient was totally cured, Maimonides revealed the reason for his bizarre behavior, and the fact that everything had been prepared and planned in advance. His goal had been to provoke Rabbi Abraham into unrestrained rage, causing enough pressure on his tear ducts to burst them open and allow the healing to occur. Seeing Maimonides' devotion, Rabbi Abraham decided to reexamine his views about his opponent, and indeed, changed his opinion completely.

Ever after that, the hearts of these two Torah giants grew closer, and they became bosom friends for the rest of their lives.

THE DECEITFUL
PATIENT

As PHYSICIAN in Egypt, Maimonides was accustomed
to analyze the urine of each patient before determin-
ing the necessary treatment. Depending on the results of the analysis, he would instruct the apothecary what
remedies to prepare for the sick adult or child.

One day a rich, haughty merchant who was skeptical about
the Rambam's ability to diagnose illness in this manner
decided to prepare a pitfall for him. What did he do? Feigning
illness, the merchant went to see Maimonides and complained
of weakness. At the consultation, he produced a bottle of don-
key urine, saying that it was his own.

After analyzing the urine, the Rambam sent for the wealthy
merchant and gave orders for him to eat daily three bags of
barley—and only barley—until further notice.

Surgery without a Scalpel

ANY TALES are told about the Rambam. As is well known, he customarily treated his patients free of charge. One day a pauper came to his clinic much later than the appointed hour—when Maimonides was already seated in the carriage on his way to the royal palace. The irate man demanded that he be examined that very instant. Since Maimonides was familiar with the pauper's malady, he prescribed a remedy without leaving the carriage and calmly asked him to return the next day at the appointed hour.

The pauper was enraged and decided to exact revenge on the Rambam. A few days later, when Maimonides was riding in the royal carriage beside the king himself, the pauper came running toward them and began shouting abuse at Maimonides: at his person, his religion, and his family. The outraged king ordered the Rambam to cut out the man's brutish heart.

When Maimonides returned home, he sought out the pauper and kindly gave him money. Every day he provided the man with milk, paid his family's rent, and supplied him with the necessary medicines. And the pauper's attitude mellowed.

Now, many days had passed when the king rode once again in his carriage accompanied by the Rambam. The same pauper came toward them, and this time he blessed, exalted, and sang praises of Maimonides, his religion, his family—and all Jews.

The king turned to the Rambam and sternly said: "Isn't this the same pauper who insulted you and whose heart I ordered you to cut out?"

"Yes, my lord king," humbly replied Maimonides.

"Then why didn't you do it?" fumed the king.

"But I did, my lord king, carry out your order. I cut out his brutish heart and endowed him with a new one: a *good* heart."

The king stared at the Rambam for a moment and then burst out laughing as he added: "So it's possible to operate even without a scalpel! This is something that I have now learned from you."

From that day on, the king held the Rambam in higher esteem than ever.

8

THE LESS SAID THE BETTER

THERE WAS once a great controversy and quarrel between the normative Jewish community and the breakaway Karaite sect living in the land of Egypt. One side said, "We are right and our way is the true way," and the other replied, "That is impossible. Our opinion is the right one and ours is the straight path."

The king, upon discovering this inflammatory matter, became angry and said: "I want no religious arguing in my country. Let the Talmudic Jews choose a rabbi and the Karaites another rabbi of their own and have them come before me for debate with each other and for my binding judgment. Thus we shall determine who is right."

Everyone acquiesced to the king's order, and a date was set for both sides to appear before him and his ministers. Of course, Maimonides was chosen to represent the mainstream Jewish community.

When the appointed day came, the Karaite rabbi arrived

punctually at the palace and was received with many honors by the royal guard. Of course, no one entered the palace with his shoes on, out of respect for the king and because the palatial floor was carpeted with expensive rugs and mats. That is why it was customary to remove one's sandals and entrust them to the doorkeepers, which is what the Karaite rabbi did.

As for the Rambam, he deliberately came late to the debate. When he finally arrived at the palace, the king and his ministers were impatiently waiting for him. Maimonides hastened to remove his sandals, but instead of handing them to the doorkeepers, he placed them under his arms. In this manner, he appeared before the king, who demanded:

"Why do you do this? Have I not enough guards to protect your footwear?"

"My lord king," slowly replied Maimonides, "when blessed Moses son of Amram climbed Mount Sinai to receive the Torah from God, he removed his sandals out of respect for that holy place. He too put them under his arms for fear that a Karaite would come and steal them."

At this remark, the Karaite rabbi sprang to his feet as though stung by a snakebite and shouted, "Your royal highness, he's telling a lie—for in those days, the Karaites did not yet exist, but only the Israelites!"

Upon hearing this, the king replied:

"Behold, you've been defeated by showing the supremacy of the Talmudic Jews over the Karaites—as they are the more ancient people. With your own mouth, you have defeated yourself."

9

A REMEDY FOR POVERTY

ONE DAY a poor and sick Jew named Samuel came to see the Rambam. The man and his wife had eight children, and he struggled to support them all by means of his humble trade as a peddler of thread and needles. Having fallen ill owing to exhaustion, he was advised by his neighbors and relatives to see the great physician.

After examining the man, Maimonides said: "With the help of God, you will be cured, but you must do as I say: As soon as you come home, take the seeds called Priest Aaron's Flower mentioned in the Torah [Numbers 17:8] and sow them in your yard. After you've done that, come and see me again in two months' time." He added: "The moment you buy the seeds, you will immediately feel well," and placing his hands on the patient's head, the Rambam gave his blessing.

Samuel returned home and sent his wife to buy the seeds called Priest Aaron's Flower. As soon as she brought them home, she directly took a hoe and, breaking the soil, sowed the seeds in the yard below their window. For three days she watered the garden beds, and on the fourth day the plant germinated and began to grow bigger and bigger.

Now it came to pass that the king of Egypt had fallen ill. The best physicians in the land came to treat him but could not determine the nature of his sickness. Nevertheless, they prescribed a medicine for him. But it only made him worse. He became critically ill, and his physicians were still unable to ascertain what his malady was. In desperation they heeded one of the king's ministers, who recommended the help of a Jewish physician: the Rambam, yet unknown to the king.

At once messengers were sent out in search of Maimonides to escort him to the royal palace. When he finally arrived, the king lay on his sickbed, breathing his last. The Rambam examined him, and after musing for several minutes, he said: "There is a flower that's called Priest Aaron's Flower. It's the only plant that can help the ailing king. He must drink an infusion of this herb three times a day, and in two days' time, he will be well enough to leave his bed."

Without delay, emissaries were sent to all the apothecary shops in the city, but none carried this rare herb. Nor could the king's emissaries find it in a single apothecary shop in the entire country. They began to search for it in impressive gardens, but after much investigation, they did not light upon it there either.

The whole royal household despaired of ever finding this good remedy, which seemingly could not be located anywhere in the kingdom. As a last resort, messengers were sent to the Jews who lived in Egypt, asking them to allow a search of their gardens. The messengers left no stone unturned, until finally they came upon Samuel's humble yard and found the herb flowering in the garden beneath his window.

With great joy they brought the flower to the king, and as soon as he drank the first infusion, he immediately felt better.

When he drank a second infusion, he felt much better, and after the third infusion, he got out of bed and jauntily strolled the grounds of his palace once more.

When the king was completely recovered, he sent his emissaries to search out the poor man whose yard held the healing plant and bring him to the palace. Then the king asked: "What do you wish in exchange for that medicine which has saved my life?"

Samuel prostrated himself before the king and said: "May the Lord of Israel bless his majesty, ruler of Egypt! I want only what the king wishes to provide for my large and destitute family."

The monarch handed Samuel a box filled with gold and silver, and after instructing a servant to escort Samuel home, he said: "Whenever there comes a time when this money is not enough for your needs, come to me and I shall give you more and more. You are worth all of my wealth, for you have saved me from the clutches of death and restored me to health."

10

SUSTAINING PEACE

LIKE ALL great figures in the world, Maimonides was surrounded by many foes who were hostile and envious. As he was friendly with the king of Egypt, the Rambam's enemies decided to damage his relationship with the sovereign. After conspiring together, they went to see Maimonides and told him that the ruler could not bear his proximity because of his bad breath. The Rambam was surprised, for he had never noticed any attempt on the kings' part to move away from him while they conversed.

At the same time, the Rambam's enemies also went to see the sovereign and told him that the insolence of his Jewish friend exceeded all bounds, for he dared complain to everyone that he could not bear the sovereign's nearness because of his bad breath. The king was dumbfounded by such an accusation and angry as well, but nevertheless he decided to test his friend, counselor, and physician.

He sent for Maimonides, and to the astonishment of all of those present, both the Rambam and the ruler arrived at their appointed place holding a white handkerchief to their mouth. To their mouth, and not to their nose—and that is how it soon became clear to both that a malicious hand was at work against Maimonides. By their manner of conducting themselves, they proved that neither one wanted to avoid the other's breath but rather to cover his own.

With this gesture, the ruler understood that it was all a plot hatched by the Rambam's foes against him.

11

THE COMFORTED
GUEST

EVERY SABBATH, the Rambam was accustomed to invite guests—especially the impoverished—to his house. On one such occasion, after pronouncing the Kiddush, Maimonides offered his guest the honor of reciting the ceremonial blessing over the wine.

But at that moment something embarrassing occurred. Due to his nervousness, the visitor inadvertently tipped over the goblet and the wine spilled on the splendid tablecloth.

Aware of his guest's distress, the Rambam immediately poured himself another goblet of wine and jostled the table intentionally—upsetting his goblet and spilling the wine.

He then stood up and said: "It seems to me that the floor here isn't very level."

Maimonides glanced at the visitor's eyes and noticed his sense of relief.

APPENDIX I

Maimonides' Major Religious-Philosophical Works

MAIMONIDES was a prolific writer from an early age. Forced to wander southern Spain with his family to escape religious persecution by the Almohads, he nevertheless composed his first two texts while still approximately in his late teens. Both works were written in Arabic, apparently in response to requests by much older, more-established scholars.

Millot ha-Higgayon (Treatise on the Art of Logic) is a treatise on logic based on Aristotle's works. Addressed to a Muslim, either real or fictitious, it presents physical, metaphysical, and ethical terms used in discussing the theory of logic. In this work Maimonides cited neither the Bible nor the Talmud and gave no hint of his Jewish identity.

Ma'amar ha-Ibbur (Essay on the Calendar) is a practical guide, replete with tables for easy comprehension, to the

Jewish calendar. Written with a minimum of jargon, it provides the rationale, mechanics, and astronomical principles for understanding Judaism's complex calendar. Maimonides' celebrated talent for erudition expressed in clear, precise writing is foreshadowed in this youthful work.

In chronological order, Maimonides' major, enduring contributions to Jewish thought and philosophy encompass the following four works:

Commentary on the Mishnah
(*Kitab al-Siraj* in Judeo-Arabic or
Perush ha-Mishnah in Hebrew)

Completed in 1168, Maimonides began composing this volume when he was twenty years old. He spent an entire decade on it, undoubtedly because of the stresses and delays of forced wandering with his family, seeking refuge throughout the Mediterranean. It was originally written in Judeo-Arabic, and various translators rendered it into Hebrew.

Embedded within this pioneering commentary are several treatises that have often been studied independently. These include Maimonides' discussion of the chapter Perek Helek in the Talmudic tractate *Sanhedrin,* which begins with the line, "All Jews have a share in the World to Come." In this treatise, Maimonides presents his view of the afterlife and his famous Thirteen Articles of Faith, which every Jew is expected to endorse.

Another highly influential, self-contained tract in Maimonides' *Commentary* is his introduction to *Pirkey Avot* (Ethics of the Fathers). Historically, this tract is known simply as *Eight Chapters;* it focuses on how to become a sage by following various psychological and ethical guidelines.

Book of Commandments (Sefer ha-Mitzvot)

Composed in Arabic and completed in 1170, the *Book of Commandments* was later described by Maimonides as having been written as an introduction to his voluminous masterpiece, the *Mishneh Torah*. According to longstanding tradition, God bestowed upon Moses at Mount Sinai 613 divine commandments for the Jewish people to follow. Yet nowhere in Judaism were these definitively enumerated or described—until Maimonides did so in this immensely influential work.

Devising fourteen organizing principles, he presented the 613 commandments in two camps. The first encompassed 248 positive commandments—corresponding to the number of organs and limbs in the human body, as if each were declaring, "Perform a commandment with me." The second camp comprised 365 negative commandments—corresponding to the days of the solar year—as if each were saying, "Do not transgress this day." Maimonides' classification has had tremendous impact on Judaism to the present day.

Mishneh Torah, or Yad ha-Hazakah (The Mighty Hand)

Written in elegant Hebrew and completed in 1180, Maimonides devoted ten years to its writing. A monumental work still studied avidly by Jews throughout the world, it catapulted its author to immediate acclaim as the greatest rabbinic thinker of his time—up to the present day.

Mishneh Torah comprises fourteen volumes and summarizes the entire Jewish legal code—including the laws regarding both Jews living in the Diaspora and those who one day would again inhabit a free, flourishing State of Israel led by the Holy Temple of Jerusalem. Writing in a concise, easy-to-understand style intended for a broad audience, Maimonides created a new way of categorizing Jewish law not found in earlier texts like the Talmud. *Mishneh Torah's* lucid conceptualizations brought a new clarity to Jewish observance. Yet, by failing to cite sources in his codification and to explain how he had resolved historically differing rabbinic opinions, Maimonides also aroused bitter criticism in his own day.

The volumes of *Mishneh Torah,* each divided into sections and subsections, are respectively entitled: (1) The Book of Knowledge, (2) The Book of Love [of God], (3) The Book of Seasons, (4) The Book of Women, (5) The Book of Holiness, (6) The Book of Utterances, (7) The Book of Seeds, (8) The Book of Temple Service, (9) The Book of Sacrifices, (10) The Book of Purity, (11) The Book of Damages, (12) The Book of Acquisition, (13) The Book of Civil Laws, and (14) The Book of Judges.

The Guide for the Perplexed

Completed in 1190, this was Maimonides' last major work and undoubtedly his most historically influential one beyond the Jewish community. Written in Judeo-Arabic over three years, its goal was to integrate the most important aspects of Greek and Arabic philosophy and science with religion—specifically Judaism—into an overarching, coherent view of human existence. Drawing heavily upon Aristotle's ideas and his own, often unique, interpretations of Jewish theology, Maimonides sought to reconcile reason and faith. The work also contained practical advice for emotional and spiritual development, ultimately leading, in Maimonides' view, to prophetic consciousness.

The *Guide's* format was in the form of an earnest lecture addressed to one person: his student and protégé Joseph ibn Aknin. Arousing tremendous interest from its inception, the

Guide was first translated into Hebrew by young Samuel ibn Tibbon in 1204. By the end of the thirteenth century, portions had also been translated into Latin and studied by such leading European philosophers as Albertus Magnus and Thomas Aquinas.

The Ten Medical Works of Maimonides

AFTER OPENING his private practice in Fustat as a physician in 1175, Maimonides composed a total of ten medical treatises. All were written in Arabic. Over the centuries, some have had greater historical impact than others. Scholars today are unsure of the precise years in which several of these books were composed. Reflecting Maimonides' belief that we comprise a unity of body, mind, and spirit, he also wrote about wellness throughout his Judaic and philosophical writings.

Indisputably, the translations and commentaries by physician Fred Rosner are the best guide to Maimonides' medical treatises. In chronological order, they comprise the following works:

Extracts from Galen, or The Art of Cure

Galen's medical writings consist of more than one hundred books. Maimonides therefore extracted what he viewed as Galen's most important medical statements and compiled them verbatim in a small work intended mainly for medical students.

Commentary on the Aphorisms of Hippocrates

In this work, Maimonides occasionally criticizes both Galen and Hippocrates when either Greek physician differs from his own viewpoint.

The Medical Aphorisms of Moses

The most voluminous of Maimonides' medical texts, this book comprises fifteen hundred aphorisms about disease presented mainly by Greco-Persian physicians. There are twenty-five chapters, each dealing with a different area of medicine, such as anatomy, pathology, fevers, hygiene, diet, and drugs. Occasionally Maimonides presents his own opinion.

Treatise on Hemorrhoids

This work was written for a nobleman, probably a member of the sultan's family. Comprising seven chapters, it provides therapeutic advice and downplays surgery as failing to address this disease's underlying cause.

Treatise on Sexual Intercourse

Written for a nephew of Saladin's who sought advice on increasing his sexual potency, this work consists mainly of recipes for foods and drugs. Maimonides also alluded to fantasy's role in affecting libido—at least for males.

Treatise on Asthma

This book was written for a patient who suffered from painful headaches that prevented him from wearing a turban. In thirteen chapters, Maimonides presented general health rules involving diet and climate, and specifically those for asthmatics. He noted that "the concern for clean air is the foremost rule in preserving the health of body and soul."

Treatise on Poisons and Their Antidotes

Among Maimonides' most popular medical treatises, this book was used as a toxicology textbook throughout the Middle Ages. It was requested by the grand vizier and supreme judge al-Fadil, seeking information on first aid for poisoning before a physician's arrival.

Regimen of Health

Its title sometimes poetically translated as "The Preservation of Youth," this work was written for Saladin's eldest son, al-Afdal, a sensualist who suffered from depression and various physical ailments. This prescient book contains a wealth of insights relating to wellness.

Discourse on the Explanation of Fits

This book is sometimes viewed as chapter 5 of the *Regimen of Health*. It was written for Saladin's eldest son, who persisted in his overindulgences and requested advice to improve his well-being.

Maimonides discussed such matters as bathing, physical exercise, laxatives, and wine—and recommended a detailed, hour-by-hour regimen for al-Afdal's daily life.

Glossary of Drug Names

This work is basically a pharmacopoeia. It comprises 405 short paragraphs containing names of drugs in Arabic, Berber, Greek, Persian, Spanish, and Syrian.

Chronology of
Maimonides' Life

1138: Maimonides (Moses ben Maimon) is born on March 30 (Passover eve) in Córdoba, Spain. His mother dies in childbirth. Until recently, scholars regarded his date of birth as 1135.

c. 1138–1147: Rabbi Maimon remarries. At least three more children are born: David, Miriam, and another sister whose name is unknown.

1147: The Maimon family flees Córdoba following invasion by the Almohads.

1151: The Maimon family flees Almería following advance by the Almohads.

c. 1147–1158: While wandering around southern Spain, Maimonides writes *Millot ha-Higgayon,* a treatise on logic, and *Ma'amar ha-Ibbur,* concerning the Jewish calendar. He also researches the writings of Talmudic sages and collects the scholarly notes of his father and Rabbi Joseph ibn Migash.

1158: Maimonides begins writing his *Commentary on the Mishnah*.

1159: The Maimon family travels to Fez, Morocco.

1160: Rabbi Maimon writes his *Letter of Consolation* to Jews of his time.

1162: Maimonides writes his *Letter on Conversion*.

1165: Maimonides is arrested by Islamic authorities for allegedly relapsing into Judaism after his (ostensible) conversion to Islam. Maimonides is released on Abul Arab ibn Moisha's favorable testimony. The Maimon family flees from Fez to Ceuta, where they voyage to the Land of Israel. Rabbi Judah ibn Shoshan, head of the Jewish community in Fez, is executed for violating his (ostensible) Muslim conversion.

1165–1166: The Maimon family sojourns several months in the Land of Israel.

1166: The Maimon family moves to Alexandria, Egypt. Within the year, they relocate to Fustat, near Cairo.

1168: Maimonides completes his *Commentary on the Mishnah* containing his Thirteen Articles of Faith.

1170: Maimonides completes his *Book of Commandments* and starts writing his *Mishneh Torah*.

1172: Maimonides writes his *Letter to Yemen*.

1174: Maimonides' brother, David, is drowned at sea.

1175: Maimonides marries the daughter (name unknown) of Rabbi Mishael Halevi of Fustat. Maimonides opens his medical practice.

1177: Maimonides receives the official title of rabbi.

1180: Maimonides completes his *Mishneh Torah*.

1185: Joseph ibn Aknin comes to Fustat to study with Maimonides.

1186: Maimonides' son, Abraham, is born.

1187: Abul Arab ibn Moisha denounces Maimonides as a traitor for violating his (ostensible) conversion to Islam, but he is saved by al-Fadil's intervention. Joseph ibn Aknin moves to Aleppo, Syria. Maimonides begins writing *The Guide for the Perplexed*. Maimonides both takes the position of court physician to al-Fadil and resumes the position of *nagid* (grand rabbi of all lands controlled by Saladin).

1190: Maimonides completes his *Guide for the Perplexed*. Rabbi Joseph ibn Aknin moves to Baghdad.

1190–1191: Maimonides writes his *Letter on Resurrection*.

1195: Rabbinic leaders of Lunel in France begin corresponding with Maimonides.

1204: Samuel ibn Tibbon completes his Hebrew translation of *The Guide for the Perplexed*. On December 13, death of Maimonides.

Glossary

Kabbalah. From the Hebrew word "to receive." Often used as a generic term for Jewish mysticism per se, it more precisely refers to esoteric thought from the late twelfth century onward.

Ketubim. Literally, "writings." These comprise the Hebrew Bible's Books of Daniel, Ecclesiastes, Esther, First and Second Chronicles, Job, Lamentations, Proverbs, Psalms, and Song of Songs.

Mishnah. The earliest postbiblical text of Jewish law and belief. It comprises six orders, each divided into tractates. It is believed to have been completed in the early third century C.E.

Oral Law. The legalistic tradition of Judaism based on the Pentateuch. After flourishing orally for centuries, it was first presented in writing in the Mishnah and later the Talmud.

Pirkey Avot. Literally, "Ethics of the Fathers." The most popular tractate of the Mishnah. It is a collection of aphorisms, governing ethics and conduct, attributed to Jewish sages who lived before the end of the second century C.E.

Rabbi. Literally, "my teacher." Originally a title for addressing a sage or a scholar, it now refers to an individual ordained according to Jewish law.

Rambam (The). The traditional Jewish appellation for Maimonides. It is an abbreviation of the words "Rabbi Moses ben Maimon."

Shema. The most important prayer in Judaism, its twice-daily recitation is a religious commandment. Its opening verse begins with the words *Sh'ma Yisrael* ("Hear O Israel") and comes from Deuteronomy 6:4.

Talmud. The summary of the Judaic oral tradition, compiled in writings by sages in Israel and Babylonia. Completed about 500 C.E., it exists today in two editions, one for each of the two centers of world Judaism of the time. The Babylonian edition is by far the more comprehensive and authoritative version. The Talmud comprises the Mishnah and the Gemara (the commentary about it).

Teshuva. "Repentance," or more broadly, return and ascent to one's source of divine origin. In Judaism, this process is accomplished by prayer, sacred study, or the performance of religious commandments or good deeds in general.

Torah. In a narrow sense, the Pentateuch (Five Books of Moses). More generally, Torah is understood to comprise the twenty-four books of the Hebrew Bible plus the Talmud.

Selected References

Alexander, Tamar, and Elena Romano, eds. *Once Upon a Time . . . Maimonides.* Translated from the Spanish and Hebrew by Rhoda Henelde Abecasis. Lancaster, Calif.: Labyrinthos, 2004.

Arbel, Ilil. *Maimonides: A Spiritual Biography.* New York: Crossroads, 2001.

Benjamin of Tudela. *The Itinerary of Benjamin of Tudela.* Translated by M. N. Adler. New York: Feldheim, 1907.

Brill, Alan. "The Phenomenology of True Dreams in Maimonides." *Dreaming* 10, no. 4 (2000): 43–54.

Cohen, Abraham, ed. *The Teachings of Maimonides.* Prolegomenon by Marvin Fox. New York: Ktav, 1968.

Hartman, David. *Torah and Philosophic Quest.* Philadelphia: Jewish Publication Society, 1976.

Heschel, Abraham Joshua. *Maimonides*. New York: Farrar, Straus & Giroux, 1982.

Hoffman, Edward. *The Heavenly Ladder: The Jewish Guide to Inner Growth*. San Francisco: Harper & Row, 1985.

————, ed. *Opening the Inner Gates*. Boston: Shambhala Publications, 1995.

————. *The Way of Splendor: Jewish Mysticism and Modern Psychology*. Updated 25th anniversary ed. Lanham, Md.: Rowman & Littlefield, 2006.

Hollister, C. Warren. *Medieval Europe: A Short History*. 7th ed. New York: McGraw-Hill, 1994.

Lowney, Chris. *A Vanished World: Muslims, Christians, and Jews in Medieval Spain*. Oxford: Oxford University Press, 2005.

Maimonides, Moses. *The Code of Maimonides*. Translated by various scholars. Bks. 2–14. New Haven: Yale University Press, 1949–2004.

————. *Crisis and Leadership: Epistles of Maimonides*. Text translation and notes by Abraham Halkin. Discussions by David Hartman. Philadelphia: Jewish Publication Society of America, 1985.

————. *The Guide for the Perplexed*. Translated and with an introduction by Shlomo Pines. Chicago: University of Chicago Press, 1963.

————. *The Guide for the Perplexed*. Translated from the original Arabic text by M. Friedlander. Introduction to the new edition by David Taffel. New York: Barnes & Noble, 2004.

————. *Mishneh Torah*. Abridged and translated from the Hebrew by Philip Birnbaum. New York: Hebrew Publishing Company, 1974.

———. *On Sexual Intercourse.* Edited and translated by Morris Gorlin. Brooklyn: Rambash, 1961.

———. *Pirkei Avot, with the Rambam's Commentary, Including Shemoneh Perakim.* Translation and notes by Eliyahu Touger. Brooklyn, N.Y.: Moznaim, 1994.

———. *The Preservation of Youth.* Translated from the original Arabic and with an introduction by Hirsch L. Gordon. New York: Philosophical Library, 1958.

———. *Rambam: The Eight Chapters, Discourse on the World to Come.* Translated and annotated by Avraham Yaakov Finkel. Scranton, Pa.: Yeshivath Beth Moshe, 1994.

Minkin, Jacob Samuel. *The World of Maimonides, with Selections from His Writings.* New York: Yoseloff, 1957.

Nuland, Sherwin B. *Maimonides.* New York: Schocken, 2005.

Rosner, Fred. *The Existence and Unity of God: Three Treatises Attributed to Moses Maimonides.* Translated and annotated from the Hebrew editions. Northvale, N.J.: Aronson, 1990.

———. "The Life of Maimonides, a Prominent Medieval Physician." *Einstein Quarterly Journal of Biological Medicine* 19 (2002): 125–28.

———, ed. and trans. *Maimonides' Commentary on the Aphorisms of Hippocrates.* Haifa, Israel: Maimonides Research Institute, 1987.

———, trans. and annotator. *Maimonides' Three Treatises on Health.* Haifa, Israel: Maimonides Research Institute, 1990.

———, trans. and annotator. *Maimonides' "Treatise on Resurrection."* Northvale, N.J.: Jason Aronson, 1997.

————. *The Medical Legacy of Maimonides.* New York: Ktav, 1998.

————. *Medicine in the "Mishneh Torah" of Maimonides.* New York: Ktav, 1984.

————, trans. and annotator. *Moses Maimonides' "Treatise on Asthma."* Haifa, Israel: Maimonides Research Institute, 1994.

————. *Sex Ethics in the Writings of Maimonides.* New York: Bloch, 1974.

————, and Samuel S. Kotteck. *Moses Maimonides: Physician, Scientist, and Philosopher.* Northvale, N.J.: Aronson, 1993.

————, and Suessman Munter, eds. and trans. *The Medical Aphorisms of Maimonides.* New York: Yeshiva University Press, 1970–71.

Seeskin, Kenneth, ed. *Maimonides.* New York: Cambridge University Press, 2005.

Stiskin, Leon D. *Letters of Maimonides.* New York: Yeshiva University Press, 1977.

Twersky, Isidore. *A Maimonides Reader.* New York: Behrman House, 1972.

Weiss, Raymond L., and Charles Butterworth, eds. *Ethical Writings of Maimonides.* New York: Dover, 1975.